Blended Learning

in Grades 4–12

For my Grandpa Ken—
Your wisdom, insight, and passion for learning inspire me.
Thank you for your endless support,
enthusiasm, and love on this journey.

Blended Learning
in Grades 4–12

Leveraging the Power of Technology to Create **STUDENT-CENTERED** Classrooms

Catlin R. Tucker

CORWIN
A SAGE Company

CORWIN
A SAGE Company

FOR INFORMATION:

Corwin
A SAGE Company
2455 Teller Road
Thousand Oaks, California 91320
(800) 233-9936
www.corwin.com

SAGE Publications Ltd.
1 Oliver's Yard
55 City Road
London EC1Y 1SP
United Kingdom

SAGE Publications India Pvt. Ltd.
B 1/I 1 Mohan Cooperative Industrial Area
Mathura Road, New Delhi 110 044
India

SAGE Publications Asia-Pacific Pte. Ltd.
3 Church Street
#10-04 Samsung Hub
Singapore 049483

Acquisitions Editor: Debra Stollenwerk
Associate Editor: Desirée A. Bartlett
Editorial Assistant: Kimberly Greenberg
Production Editor: Amy Joy Schroller
Copy Editor: Sarah J. Duffy
Typesetter: C&M Digitals (P) Ltd.
Proofreader: Bonnie Moore
Indexer: Sylvia Coates
Cover Designer: Scott Van Atta
Permissions Editor: Adele Hutchinson

Printed in the United States of America

Library of Congress Cataloging-in-Publication Data

Tucker, Catlin R.

Blended learning in grades 4-12: leveraging the power of technology to create student-centered classrooms /Catlin R. Tucker.

p. cm.

Includes bibliographical references and index.

ISBN 978-1-4522-4086-2 (pbk. : alk. paper)
1. Student-centered learning. 2. Blended learning. I. Title.

LB1027.23.T84 2012
371.3—dc23   2012016181

This book is printed on acid-free paper.

MIX
Paper from responsible sources
FSC www.fsc.org   FSC® C012947

17 18 19 10 9 8 7 6

Contents

Web Tools Contents

 Additional materials and resources related to *Blended Learning in Grades 4–12* can be found at www.corwin.com/blended learning4-12.

Web Tools

Chapter	Tools
3. The Role of the Teacher in a Blended Learning Model	• Blackboard • Moodle • Edmodo • Schoology • Collaborize Classroom
6. English Language Arts	• Glogster • Storybird • Blabberize • Animoto • Wix • Tiki-Toki • Read, Write, Think • Pixton • Gliffy
7. History/Social Studies	• Penzu • Photovisi • History.com • History Wiz • The Library of Congress

Chapter	Tools
	• American Rhetoric • Wordle • Lino • Churchill Museum and Cabinet War Rooms • Pen.io • My Fake Wall • Study Blue • PicMonkey
8. Science	• Corkboard.me • HurricaneKatrina.com • Weebly • UNISYS • National Geographic • Virtual Teacher Aid • Mongabay • Biology Junction • Queeky • Lucid Chart • ProConLists.com
9. Math	• Wall Wisher • National Center for Education Statistics Kids' Zone • Khan Academy • Google Docs • Educreations • Survey Monkey • Creately
11. Assessing Work Online	• Rubistar • Google Forms

Resources

Resource 5.1. Dos and Don'ts of Student Communication Online
Resource 5.2. Strong Sentence Starters
Resource 5.3. Example Online Student Code of Conduct Agreement
Resource 5.4. Example Safe Space Reflection Form
Resource 5.5. Avoid Mechanical Missteps in Online Communication
Resource 5.6. Say Something Substantial
Resource 5.7. Eight Intriguing Exit Strategies That Continue the Conversation

Book Study Questions

Additional English Curriculum

Common Core State Standards: Upper Elementary English

Example Writing Task: Do You Like the Secondary Characters in Lewis Carroll's *Alice in Wonderland*?

Example Writing Task: In the Book *The Black Stallion* by Walter Farley, How Does Alec Ramsey Grow and Develop as a Character?

Example Writing Task: Home Sweet Home—Imagine You Live in This House . . . Tell Your Story!

Common Core State Standards: Middle School English

Example Discussion Topic: *Little Women*—Characters Revealed

Example Discussion Topic: *The Dark Is Rising*—Inspired by British Myth, History, Tradition, and Legends About King Arthur

Example Writing Task: Your Road Not Taken

Common Core State Standards: High School English

Example Writing Task: *Of Mice and Men* Essay—Do You Think George Made the Right Decision When He Shot Lennie?

Example Writing Task: *The Grapes of Wrath* Essay—Family Is Necessary to Survival

Example Writing Task: Getting Creative With F. Scott Fitzgerald's *The Great Gatsby*

Preface

Why Did I Write This Book?

I wish I could say my decision to adopt a blended learning model stemmed from a desire to be innovative and progressive. To be honest, it came from a place of desperation. I was drowning in work. Larger class sizes, overwhelming stacks of grading, and more pressure from administration to prepare students for "high-stakes" standardized exams were the true catalysts that led me to adopt a blended learning model.

I was hesitant, even skeptical, at first. I worried about student access to technology, the time required to facilitate online work, and how I would create a virtual safe space to support respectful dialogue.

I had eight years' experience teaching high school English in the classroom and three years' experience teaching online college-level writing courses. My goal was to blend the best of both worlds—the face-to-face interaction of the classroom with the flexibility of online discussions, collaboration, and group work—in order to enhance my effectiveness and combat the growing number of pain points afflicting the teaching profession.

I have learned a great deal about the Web tools available to me over the last few years. And I have explored the limitless potential of online discussions as a foundation for myriad online assignments. I evolved from asking analytical questions about literature to using my learning platform to support collaborative group work, creative writing, peer editing, student-driven projects, and standardized test practice. As a result, I feel more empowered. I realize that technology cannot replace me, but it can make me more effective, decrease my grading load, and teach my students critical 21st century skills they will use long after they have left my class.

hat Is the Purpose of This Book?

ıv.ost teachers are so overworked it is daunting to imagine shifting to a blended learning model. This book presents a clear path teachers can take to adopt a blended learning model that works for them and their students.

Many college-level texts on blended learning focus on the pedagogy, theory, structural design, and budgetary issues at the heart of a blended learning model. This book was written for teachers in upper elementary through high school, so the focus of this text is practical application of these theories in Grade 4–12 classrooms.

Why should a teacher buy this book?

1. It advocates for a teacher-designed blended learning model with concrete strategies, ready-to-use resources, and examples grounded in the Common Core State Standards.

2. It shows teachers how they can use an online environment to give every student a voice, increase engagement, drive higher-order thinking, and make homework an interactive experience instead of a solitary practice.

3. Teachers will learn how to integrate technology into their existing curriculum in order to build community and create a student-centered classroom that challenges students to be active participants in the learning process.

This book will also provide professional development instructors, instructional designers, curriculum specialists, administrators, and credential programs with resources needed to support upper elementary through high school teachers in effectively shifting to a blended learning model.

The theme of the student-centered classroom is woven throughout this book because the ultimate goal of using technology to complement work done in class is to shift the focus in the classroom from the teacher to the students. Technology can be used to introduce information and engage students in discussions and collaborative group work that have traditionally required large amounts of class time. This frees up precious class time to focus on activities that utilize the potential of the group.

How Is This Book Organized?

Chapters 1 and 2 describe the changing landscape of education, identify 21st century skills that students today need to be successful, and define what the term *blended learning* means. This introduction lays the foundation for subsequent chapters, which provide strategies, concrete resources, and examples.

Chapters 3 through 5 cover topics that will help teachers get started with a blended learning model. Chapter 3 focuses on the teacher's role in a blended learning model, with a discussion of learning platforms, facilitation roles, and weaving the two mediums—face-to-face and online—together. Chapter 4 is about the art of asking questions that successfully drive dynamic discussions online. It includes tips and strategies teachers can use to design engaging online discussion questions and topics for students. This chapter covers question types that drive discussions as well as question types that kill conversations. I have designed a variety of example questions for each of the four subjects covered in the Common Core State Standards: English, history/social studies, science, and math. Chapter 5 describes a clear strategy for building relationships online and teaching students how to contribute in a respectful, supportive, and substantive way. This chapter walks teachers through the best practices for creating a virtual safe space, establishing expectations, and fostering relationships online. I encourage teachers to begin with a solid foundation to avoid problems online (e.g., cyberbullying) and raise awareness about netiquette.

Chapters 6 through 9 are subject-specific chapters that focus on the four subject areas covered in the Common Core State Standards: English, history/social studies, science, and math. Each of these chapters provides examples of online discussions and activities that address the Standards for upper elementary school (Grades 4–5), middle school (Grades 6–8), and high school (Grades 9–12). I have clearly identified the Standards associated with each online task.

Each online example is followed by three lesson ideas for student-centered in-class activities that build on the work done online. These activities are not complete lesson plans; rather, they are designed to inspire teachers who want to draw online work back into the classroom to create student-centered learning opportunities. For those of us with little technology in our classrooms, I suggest low-tech strategies for extending online work done at home back into the physical classroom. For those with 1-to-1 programs, computer labs, or laptops, I offer suggestions for incorporating technology into these student-centered activities. Throughout Chapters 6 through 9, I include information in the sidebars about the Web tools I mention. You will find the URL, a brief description of the tool, and information about costs associated with using it. I have tried to focus on Web tools that are free or have a lower cost for educators.

Chapter 10 discusses the flipped classroom, which is an instructional model that falls under the umbrella of blended learning. In this model the work traditionally done in the classroom and the work done at home are flipped. Students view videos of lectures, demonstrations, documentaries, and other forms of media at home, then class time is used to apply that knowledge. The goal is to maximize class time to facilitate hands-on practice in the classroom and shift the focus from the teacher to the students. I encourage teachers who flip their classrooms to wrap the content students view at home in a dynamic discussion or debate, which improves retention and encourages students to demonstrate higher-order thinking.

Finally, Chapter 11 ends the book with a discussion of how teachers can assess the work done online, while making the points for virtual work visible. Because many teachers are feeling pressure to prepare students for standardized exams, there is a section dedicated to using the online space to prepare students for these high-stakes tests without sacrificing class time. I also designed and included a collection of rubrics that are anchored in the Common Core State Standards to aid teachers in assessing online work more efficiently. These can be used as is or adapted for individual teachers' needs.

Each chapter ends with a summary and a collection of study questions. Because I believe discussion is central to learning, I designed questions to encourage further conversations about the topics covered in this book. They may serve as a helpful guide for school districts, credential programs, and groups of educators completing a book study of this text. These questions are intended to invite reflection and produce discussions about how educators might implement, adapt, or build on the ideas presented.

Companion Website

In addition to this text, there is a companion website available at www.corwin.com/blendedlearning4-12 with the following information hosted online:

- *Web Tools.* Information, hyperlinks, and ideas for using them in the classroom.
- *Resources.* A PDF of each resource in the book is available for download.
- *Chapter Questions.* Each set of questions appears online.
- *Additional English Curriculum.* I have designed additional online discussions and student-centered activities since this is my area of expertise. These are provided online for language arts teachers who are interested in more blended instruction lesson ideas.

I hope this book will spread awareness about a teacher-designed approach to blended learning that does not reduce student-teacher face time, like many hybrid models being adopted by school districts desperate to save money. The pedagogical approaches to teaching described in this book, combined with the lessons and best practice tips, can be applied to a variety of blended learning scenarios regardless of the school you teach at or the learning platform you use.

Acknowledgments

Corwin would like to thank the following individuals for taking the time to provide their editorial feedback:

Melody Aldrich
English Teacher/Department
    Chair
Poston Butte High School
San Tan Valley, AZ

Jim Anderson
Principal
Andersen Junior High School
Chandler, AZ

Judy Brunner
Clinical Faculty, Author, and
    Consultant
Missouri State University and
    Instructional Solutions Group
Springfield, MO

David Callaway
Seventh-Grade Social Studies
    Teacher
Rocky Heights Middle School
Highlands Ranch, CO

Cathy Bonneville Hix
K–12 Social Studies Specialist
Arlington County Public Schools
Arlington, VA

About the Author

 **Catlin R. Tucker** teaches English language arts at Sonoma County's Windsor High School and online college-level writing courses. She is a Google Certified Teacher who complements her in-class instruction with online discussions and group collaboration using a variety of Web 2.0 tools in a unique teacher-designed blended learning curriculum. She writes an education blog (catlintucker.com), leads professional development, designs curriculum, and frequently speaks at education technology events. Catlin earned her bachelor's degree from the University of California, Los Angeles, and English Teaching Credential and education master's from the University of California, Santa Barbara.

1

The 21st Century
Classroom

The addition of technology does not necessarily equate to a 21st century classroom; however, technology can be the vehicle used to hook student interest and develop relevant skills needed to be successful beyond school. As the job market changes and the demand for technologically savvy workers grows, providing students with the ability to understand and use key technology tools in school is becoming critical. Currently, 50% of today's jobs require technology skills and that number is expected to grow to 77% in the next 10 years (Arnold Group, 2011). When students leave high school, they enter an increasingly digital world. A growing number of jobs will require that applicants know how to work remotely, dialogue online with coworkers, work collaboratively using tools like Google Docs and wikis, and communicate via e-mail, Skype, and Twitter. The globalization of the workplace requires a skill set that many students are not taught in school. In fact, the absence of technology in school creates a disconnect between the students' lives outside of the classroom, which are often saturated in technology, and the learning taking place inside the classroom.

A survey conducted in May 2011 found that 94% of students believe learning and mastering technology will improve their educational and career opportunities; however, just 39% say their high school is currently meeting their technology expectations (CDW, 2011). If students see the value in learning how to use technology effectively, then teachers can create buy-in and gain student interest if they teach these skills in parallel with their existing subject matter.

Crossing the Digital Divide

For those teachers and schools lucky enough to have the funding for iPads, 1-to-1 computer programs, and video cameras, this new digital frontier in education has been easier to explore. But for the vast majority of teachers, myself included, the digital divide and inequities in access require them to be innovative and resourceful if they want to use technology.

That said, I do not think lack of access can be an excuse not to incorporate technology into our teaching. If teachers are not providing students with opportunities to engage in conversations online, work with media to enhance communication, and learn to express themselves digitally, then we are not truly preparing them with the skill set needed for life beyond high school.

Teachers always ask me, "What do you do if a kid doesn't have access to technology?" Ironically, this question is often asked at an education technology conference where the goal is successful integration of technology. My answer: "Find them access." Libraries, on campus or in the community, are often a resource for computers and Internet connections. Friends or family may have computers students can use. A report by the Pew Internet and American Life Project "reveals that 93% of teens ages 12–17 go online" either at home, at school, or at the local library (Pew Research Center, 2012, para. 1). Those students without computers and/or reliable Internet access at home—a hurdle for many rural communities—are already disenfranchised. If we do not find a way to get them online and teach them to use technology effectively, they will remain disenfranchised.

We are at a breaking point where students who do not have access are not being served by the system. A press release from the Arnold Group (2011) states,

> In the U.S., approximately 9.5 million students are digitally excluded outside of their schools. According to the Federal Reserve, these students have a high school graduation rate six to eight points lower than those who have home access to the Internet. (para. 4)

In my opinion, this is quickly developing into the next civil rights issue. Those families without access to technology and/or the Internet are not privy to huge amounts of information, basic services, and countless opportunities. We have to find a way to empower students with technology regardless of their socioeconomic status.

The number of students with access should significantly increase as programs like the $4 billion public-private partnership announced by the Federal Communications Commission (FCC) in November 2011 are implemented. The FCC plans to make "high-speed Internet access and computers more affordable for more than 25 million mainly low-income Americans" (Vaughn, 2011, para. 1). Low-income families that qualify will be able to get Internet for $9.95 per month and refurbished computers for $150, which has the potential to have a huge impact on access to technology in lower socioeconomic areas.

Developing 21st Century Skills Is Critical to Future Success

The skills and knowledge needed to be successful today are different from those needed 50, 20, or even 10 years ago. As the global marketplace rapidly evolves, the landscape of education must also evolve to adequately prepare students for life beyond secondary school. Companies want students who

- possess creativity,
- communicate effectively,
- think critically,
- solve problems and find creative solutions,
- work collaboratively,
- leverage technology successfully,
- demonstrate the ability to be innovative.

To learn, practice, and master these skills, students must be put at the center of learning. This is why I emphasize the importance of a *student-centered classroom* throughout this book. Students cannot be passive observers if they are to learn 21st century skills; rather, they must be active participants in the learning process. They must be challenged with real-life situations and problems. They need to learn to work with their peers collaboratively and communicate effectively to find creative solutions. Today's students will enter a rapidly changing world that will require them to think fast and use their peers as resources. This will be much easier to do if they have been enthusiastic participants in their education.

Technology provides the time and flexibility needed to shift from the traditional model of instruction, where the teacher stands at the front of the classroom disseminating information, to a more collaborative model, which values each voice in the classroom as an important component in the collective learning process.

As Andrew Churches (2009) discusses in *Bloom's Digital Taxonomy*, "an increasing influence on learning is the impact of collaboration in its various forms. These are often facilitated by digital media and are increasingly a feature of our digital classrooms" (p. 3). This digital media allows all ideas to be shared and voices heard, which is critical for true collaboration. Effective communication is essential for students to work successfully with others on an intellectual task to create or produce something. The variety of barriers that impede discussion in the classroom—discussion dominators, shy or anxious students, lack of time needed to process, not enough time to hear all contributions—are eliminated when discussions take place, in part, online. The value of discussion as a critical component to learning is emphasized throughout this book and discussed specifically in Chapter 2.

Teachers who incorporate collaborative tools into their teaching by using learning platforms (discussed in Chapter 3), discussion boards, wikis, or blogs provide students with critical exposure to new technology and support the cultivation of collaboration and communication skills. Although collaboration is often mentioned as an increasingly important skill, many students do not feel they are being given academic opportunities to develop this ability. In a survey of high school students, 59% of students said they use technology to communicate with other students, but just 23% said they use it to collaborate with other students. Many students communicate informally on social networking sites, but it is necessary to teach them how to communicate respectfully, supportively, and substantively online to collaborate effectively on academic tasks. Chapter 5 provides resources to aid teachers in making their expectations for communication clear and provides strategies for teaching students how to contribute to a conversation in a meaningful way. Once students have learned how to communicate online, then they can begin to collaborate effectively.

Technology can provide equity of voice and engage students in more complex tasks that require time, communication, and collaboration. As I began to plan my in-class lessons to complement the work done online, I was able to prioritize these skills and design creative activities that required students to think critically, problem solve, demonstrate intellectual agility, take initiative, communicate both orally and in writing, and collaborate. The integration of online work into my curriculum allowed me the time and flexibility to create a more student-centered classroom.

What Does the 21st Century Classroom Look Like?

The traditional classroom is usually set up with rows of desks facing a board at the front of the room. Students have pen and paper ready to take notes as the teacher lectures and projects information onto the board. In this classroom the information flows from the teacher to the students. The teacher stands at the front of the room with all students facing him or her. Students are asked to sit quietly and refrain from talking to one another for most of the period. Cell phones and other wireless devices are turned off and stored in backpacks where they will not distract from the learning.

In his article "Create! Communicate! Collaborate! The 21st-Century Learner Is Here—Is Your Classroom Ready?" Mark Stevens (2011) remarks,

> The typical physical building where all learning takes place has remained largely the same over the last 100 years. We live with the reality that the same structures of brick, mortar, and steal will continue to greet us each morning. The great news is that 21st-century learning can take place in every school. (para. 2)

He stresses that the learning environments are transformed into 21st century classrooms not by the addition of gadgets, but rather by educators "employing today's technologies to make material accessible and engaging."

In contrast to the traditional teacher-centered classrooms of the past, the 21st century classroom is student centered, prioritizing student interaction, communication, and collaboration. Students must face each other to work effectively. Instead of the teacher projecting information, students use wireless devices to conduct research and discuss the information they find. Use of wireless devices is encouraged to ensure that students learn how to use the technology for academic purposes. This classroom may appear more hectic as students have conversations and move around to work together. The flow of information in this classroom bounces from student to student, teacher to student, and student to teacher. The collective potential of the group is valued and leveraged, making it possible to create a student-centered learning experience.

Student-Centered Classroom

Student-centered learning

> is broadly based on constructivism as a theory of learning, which is built on the idea that learners must construct and reconstruct knowledge in order to learn effectively, with learning being most effective when, as part of an activity, the learner experiences constructing a meaningful product. (Attard, Di Iorio, Geven, & Santa, 2010, p. 2)

This approach to learning is grounded in the following principles:

- Students must play an active instead of a passive role in learning.
- "Deep learning and understanding" (p. 2) must be valued and emphasized, thus quality must be paramount to quantity.
- Students must have an increased "responsibility and account-ability" in the learning process.
- Learners should develop an "increased sense of autonomy" (p. 2) and independence. "Choice is central to effective learning" (p. 3).
- Curriculum should be customized and differentiated to better meet the needs of all students. The one-size-fits-all approach does not work.
- Teachers must honor different learning styles and appeal to student interests to effectively engage them.
- Teachers and students must rely on one another, and their relationship must be based on mutual respect.
- Teachers and students must take time to reflect on the teaching and learning process.

Within this model, students enjoy more freedom and control over the direction of their learning. As a result students feel their voices and contributions are valued, they are motivated to play a more active role in their education, and they feel empowered by their learning.

As Dr. Richard Felder (n.d.), from North Carolina State University, states, "Student-centered teaching methods shift the focus of activity from the teacher to the learners. These methods include active learning, in which students solve problems, answer questions, formulate questions of their own, discuss, explain, debate, or brainstorm during class" (para. 2).

Student-centered instruction in the physical classroom can build naturally on the work done online if educators use the online space to create a community of inquiry. The community-of-inquiry framework, much like the student-centered approach, values active and cooperative learning that requires students to engage with the curriculum. They are encouraged to question, work together, and problem solve. To cultivate these skills educators must shift from a lecture-based approach, which is teacher centered, to an inquiry model that is student centered. A more in-depth explanation of the community of inquiry as it relates to online communities is included in Chapter 2.

The student-centered classroom is one in which students regularly engage with their peers in collaborative inquiry-based activities and assignments. As Leo Jones (2007), from Cambridge University, states, "In a student-centered class, students don't depend on their teacher all the time, waiting for instructions, words of approval, correction, advice, or praise"; instead they "value each other's contributions; they cooperate, learn from each other, and help each other" (p. 2). Students work in groups, in pairs, or alone in this type of classroom, depending on the assignment and the learning outcomes.

Although teachers play a critical role in both the traditional and the student-centered classroom, the skill sets required by each are different. The teacher in a student-centered classroom acts as a facilitator who is "responsible for helping students work independently, monitoring them while they're working together and giving them feedback afterward" (Jones, 2007, p. 25). Letting go and allowing students to work together can be challenging. It requires patience as students learn to see each other as resources, but it helps them build confidence in their ability to tackle problems together. Students become empowered when they are able to drive their own learning, and the outcomes are much more meaningful.

This book focuses on highlighting the ways that integrating technology into the traditional curriculum can create more opportunities to engage students more actively, creating a student-centered classroom.

Chapter Summary

The world is rapidly changing, and technology is quickly permeating most facets of life. Students today must leave school with the 21st century skills needed to be successful beyond the classroom. These skills are more easily taught when teachers integrate technology that supports communication and collaboration. It can be challenging to teach these skills in a classroom with 30 or more students. The lack of equity in their contributions and limited amount of time are just two impediments to engaging students in dynamic discussions and collaborative group work. However, teachers who adopt collaborative technology and use it to complement their existing curriculum can provide the time and space to engage students in more meaningful assignments.

Technology can make it possible for teachers to shift the flow of information in a classroom to create a student-centered classroom that requires students to take a more active role in their education. The student-centered classroom is one characterized by increased engagement, student responsibility, respectful communication, and effective collaboration. In this classroom, teachers serve as facilitators.

The goal of this book is to help teachers effectively integrate collaborative online tools that support dynamic discussions and group work, thus creating a student-centered experience both in the classroom and online.

Book Study Questions

1. What role do you think technology should play in education? How can technology add to and/or distract from learning? Do you think schools today are effectively preparing students for college and careers?

2. What technology do you or the teachers in your district currently use with students? What are the benefits of this technology? What challenges have you encountered? What skills are your students developing as a result of using this technology?

3. How do you define 21st century skills? What qualities or abilities would you add to the list provided in this chapter? What role should technology play in cultivating these skills?

4. What issues related to access do you face at your school or in your district? How can you overcome these obstacles to ensure students have access to technology? Are there computer labs on campus or at local libraries that students can use?

5. How can lack of access disenfranchise students and their families in your community? Will the public-private partnerships

offering computers and Internet to low-income families help your students? How can you raise awareness at your school or in your community about these opportunities?

6. Why are communication and collaboration so important to learning? How do you currently teach these skills? How can you use technology to provide more opportunities to develop these skills? In addition to work in the classroom, why is teaching online communication and collaboration important?

7. How is your room set up? Is it easy to facilitate group work in your physical space? What changes could you make in your physical classroom to encourage more communication and collaboration? What is your policy on mobile devices?

8. Is your classroom teacher centered, student centered, or a combination? What are the benefits and challenges of each model? How can using technology create more opportunities for you to shift away from the traditional paradigm to engage students more actively in the learning process?

References

Arnold Group. (2011). *Microsoft commits to bringing technology access to 1 million low-income youth.* Retrieved from http://www.thearnoldgroup.us/company/press-release.html

Attard, A., Di Iorio, E., Geven, K., & Santa, R. (2010). *Student-centered learning toolkit.* Brussels, Belgium: Lifelong Learning Programme. Retrieved from http://www.esu-online.org/pageassets/projects/projectarchive/100814-SCL.pdf

CDW. (2011). *2011 CDW-G 21st-century classroom report.* Available from http://newsroom.cdw.com/features/feature-06-27-11.html

Churches, Andrew. "Bloom's Taxonomy." Edorigami. 4 Jan 2009. Web. http://edorigami.wikispaces.com/file/view/bloom%27s+Digital+taxonomy+v3.01.pdf

Felder, R. M. (n.d.). *Student-centered teaching and learning.* Retrieved from http://www4.ncsu.edu/unity/lockers/users/f/felder/public/Student-Centered.html

Jones, L. (2007). *The student-centered classroom.* Cambridge, UK: Cambridge University Press. Retrieved from http://www.cambridge.org/other_files/downloads/esl/booklets/Jones-Student-Centered.pdf

Pew Research Center. (2012). *Teen and young adult Internet use.* Retrieved from http://pewresearch.org/millennials/teen-internet-use-graphic.php

Stevens, M. (2011, August). Create! Communicate! Collaborate! The 21st-century learner is here—Is your classroom ready? *NEA Today.* Retrieved from http://www.nea.org/home/1814.htm

Vaughn, A. (2011, November 9). FCC launching $4-billion program to narrow digital divide. *Los Angeles Times.* Retrieved from http://www.latimes.com/

2

Blended Learning

What Is Blended Learning?

The term *blended learning* is shrouded in mystery because it refers to a relatively new approach to instruction that has been implemented in a variety of ways in a myriad of educational settings.

Blended learning weaves various instructional mediums into a cohesive whole. This broad, amorphous term refers to the spectrum of teaching modes that combine traditional face-to-face instruction with an online component. This integrated approach to teaching has been borne of both necessity and increased access to technology.

The necessity for a better solution to the growing education crisis in the United States is leading many educators and institutions to this hybrid style of instruction. Growing class sizes, dwindling resources, and increasing pressure to teach to high-stakes standardized exams are causing many teachers to feel overwhelmed and disillusioned with the teaching profession. The demand placed on teachers to do more with less has led many to embrace this new model of instruction.

Many school districts faced with drastic budget cuts have implemented this hybrid model to service more students while saving money on maintaining brick-and-mortar schools that are expensive to run 5 days a week, 10 months a year.

In Florida, e-learning labs are emerging that rely on computers to teach curriculum in a lab with only a facilitator or paraprofessional monitoring students' progress. These facilitators are not trained in the subject area and are present only to monitor behavior and deal with computer issues. Currently, there are "7,000 students in Miami–Dade County Public Schools enrolled in a program in which core subjects are taken in classrooms with no teacher" (Herrera, 2011, para. 3). These learning labs are one example of how school districts are using technology to deal with class size mandates. However, many teachers resist this move toward online learning because they feel it devalues the role of the teacher as an integral part of the learning process.

Teachers can, however, play an active role in deciding how and to what extent computers, technology, and online education platforms integrate with their current curriculum. It is my belief that the teachers who embrace rather than resist technology can have an influential voice in deciding how it is blended into the educational setting as this trend continues.

Blended learning provides teachers and students with flexibility. Teachers can design lessons that weave the best of traditional instruction with the unique benefits of an online component to achieve optimal learning outcomes for all students. This frees teachers from the perpetual race against the bell. Instead of jamming huge amounts of curriculum into one class period, teachers can complement their in-class instruction with an online component to make work done at home more meaningful. Lessons can begin in class and continue online and vice versa. The trick for the instructor is to weave these two instructional mediums together. The topic of weaving will be discussed further in Chapter 3.

The blended learning model is malleable, allowing individual instructors to shape how it complements their curriculum. Teachers can tailor this model of instruction to best meet their students' diverse needs. For example, students who often feel anxious or shy about speaking in front of peers can benefit from asynchronous—occurring at different times—online discussions, activities, and group work. This provides time for students to consider a question or topic, articulate a response, and read the responses posted by their peers. For many students this gives them an equal voice in discussions without feeling the pressure to speak in front of the entire class in real time.

Many schools have found that providing students with information online—especially now that digital texts and resources are more readily available—and then using face-to-face interactions to discuss that information and work in collaborative groups to apply the information is a better use of class time.

The online component of a blended learning model can support a wide range of student-driven projects and assignments that are often neglected in traditional classrooms due to time constraints and a general lack of student focus. Involvement in a project can take place asynchronously online, allowing students to participate in a time and space that is convenient and comfortable for them.

The second factor leading to this trend in education is the proliferation of technology in our society and the mastery of this technology by students. Even teachers with limited technology in their classrooms can harness and leverage the mobile technology brought into the classroom by their students to create a blended learning environment.

In the *2011 CDW-G 21st Century Classroom Report*, a survey found that 86% of students said they use technology more outside of the classroom than in class and 94% of students said they use technology to study or work on class assignments at home (CDW, 2011). These numbers sharply contrast with the 46% of faculty who said they regularly assign homework that requires the use of technology. According to this survey conducted in May 2011, the vast majority of students are using technology at home for academic purposes; however, students are electing to use much of this technology on their own. Students recognize the value of technology to succeed in school, and the majority have access, which means teachers can use that access to design homework that extends beyond traditional pen-and-paper assignments to engage a growing number of technologically savvy students.

As budgets shrink and workloads increase, blended learning offers teachers the opportunity to break the traditional mold and create a hybrid learning environment that fosters collaboration, provides much-needed flexibility, and prioritizes student-centered instruction.

Six Common Blended Learning Models Currently in Use

In *The Rise of K–12 Blended Learning*, Michael B. Horn and Heather Staker (n.d.) discuss the six most common blended learning models currently in use. Here is a brief description of them:

1. *Face-to-Face Driver.* The teacher still delivers the majority of curriculum. The online learning element is used on a "case-by-case basis to supplement or remediate, often in the back of the

classroom or in a technology lab" (p. 4). This model is quickly evolving beyond remediation to allow teachers to integrate Web 2.0 technology to more fully engage students in online discussions, activities, and projects beyond the physical classroom.

2. *Rotation.* As the name suggests, this model rotates on a fixed schedule between learning online and learning in the classroom. This blends self-paced work online with face-to-face instruction. In this model, the "face-to-face teacher usually oversees the online work" (p. 4).

3. *Flex.* This model relies on "an online platform that delivers most of the curricula" (p. 4). Tutorial sessions or small-group instruction with teachers can be incorporated to allow time for students to access instructors, but the majority of work is done virtually. This model is used in "many dropout-recovery and credit-recovery blended programs" (p. 4).

4. *Online Lab.* Learning takes place on a school campus in a computer lab. Online teachers deliver curriculum via an online learning platform. These computer labs are monitored by paraprofessionals who are not trained in the subject area, but rather are present to deal with discipline or technology issues. Many students taking an online lab class will "also take traditional courses and have typical block schedules" (p. 5).

5. *Self-Blend.* This model "encompasses any time students choose to take one or more courses online to supplement their traditional school's catalog" (p. 6). The online learning element is always completely remote, not in an on-campus lab. Students decide on the combination of traditional classes and online classes in this model.

6. *Online Driver.* Both the online learning platform and the traditional teacher deliver content. The majority of work is done remotely, but face-to-face meetings with an instructor are incorporated as either an optional or required element depending on the program.

Emerging Blended Learning Model: Teacher-Designed Blend

This book focuses on an emerging variation of the Face-to-Face model that I call the Teacher-Designed Blend, which still values the teacher as the primary deliverer of content and designer of curriculum. However, in this spin on Model 1, online work expands beyond remediation or credit makeup to better serve all students. An online learning platform is integrated into the traditional curriculum to complement in-class work. The online learning platform can be used to support discussions related to curriculum, introduce multimedia, and facilitate student-driven projects.

The Teacher-Designed Blend offers teachers control over their curriculum and delivery, while still providing students with an online component that is more flexible and offers true opportunities for dynamic discussion and collaboration with peers. The ultimate goal of a blended learning class should be twofold: (1) allow the teacher to continue working directly with students and (2) use an online component to develop a learning community that works together to discover knowledge.

Growing online courses and virtual classrooms contribute to an atmosphere of skepticism and fear among seasoned educators who have spent years perfecting their craft. They fear that the use of technology diminishes their role and devalues the actual presence of the teacher.

The effectiveness of online courses and distance learning has been questioned, but research suggests that they can be successful for independent, motivated, and self-disciplined students. The flexibility of these courses make them attractive, but they do require students to push themselves to make the most of the experience. It does not necessarily work as well for students who are less mature, motivated, and disciplined. For them, we still need teachers to provide the necessary inspiration and structure.

The Teacher-Designed Blend is a logical alternative to online and distance courses only, or to in-class instruction only. It supplements traditional classroom instruction but does not replace it, giving both teachers and students the best of both worlds.

Ask students why they love a particular class. Chances are they will mention a teacher they connected with, who inspired them, or a teacher who explained the subject so they "got it," or understood what the teacher was trying to communicate. Teachers add experience, expertise, personality, compassion, and variety to a class in a way that a computer alone never could. Unlike online courses, the blended learning model values the teacher's face-to-face interactions with students as crucial to the success of the course.

Teaching is evolving, and technology is an important part of that evolution. Students deserve to learn using the technology they will inevitably encounter when they enter college and/or the workforce.

It is important today that teachers teach digital literacy, digital writing, and virtual citizenship in conjunction with traditional subject matter.

Although the ideas and strategies presented in this book can be applied to a variety of blended learning scenarios, this book focuses on the Teacher-Designed Blend. The goal is to empower teachers with the knowledge and resources needed to integrate technology and online tools to be more effective and engage more students to improve learning.

10 Benefits of a Blended Learning Model

1. Save Time

Teachers spend hours each week creating, copying, collating, stapling, and hole-punching handouts, assignments, and activity sheets for students. Much of this time is eliminated when a teacher transitions to an online education platform where handouts can be uploaded and attached to questions, topics, and assignment descriptions.

2. Save Money

Copy machines, ink, paper, and repairs cost school districts thousands of dollars annually (monthly for some larger districts). Most school sites spend five to nine cents per copy. My school district currently spends seven cents a copy, which means one handout for each of my 164 students costs $11.50.

In less fortunate districts, teachers are forced to spend hundreds—if not thousands—of dollars of their own money to supplement classroom resources.

Teachers can save money and paper by posting assignments, directions, notes, and reading materials online. This also helps "organizationally challenged" students who tend to lose or misplace everything handed to them. All information is in one easily accessed place.

3. Spend Less Time Grading

Online work frees teachers from their role as the only source of information and feedback. When students engage in dynamic online discussions and collaborative group work, they become valued resources in the class. They ask each other clarifying questions, compliment strong ideas, provide suggestions for improvement, and offer alternative perspectives. This also allows for improved student engagement and immediate peer feedback.

It is easy to eliminate worksheets that have limited potential to inspire, when students are actively participating in dynamic online discussions related to the curriculum.

4. Spend More Time in Class Doing What You Love

With less time spent in copy centers and grading paperwork, teachers can focus on designing innovative learning opportunities that employ the nearly limitless resources available on the Internet. The classroom can become a more student-centered environment because there is less pressure to cover all the content in the physical classroom. The online space can be used to introduce information and give students a place to have conversations about that information. This allows more flexibility in the classroom because students can spend more time working in collaborative groups to do creative tasks related to the subject matter.

5. Increase One-on-One Interactions With Students

Teachers can use online tools to engage in conversations with students that they may not normally have. Some students are shy or anxious about speaking with a teacher in class; online discussions give students easy access to one another and the teacher. They can post questions and get answers outside the confines of a normal school day, in a setting familiar to them.

6. Give Students Opportunities to Practice Standardized Exams Online

Most teachers do not want to spend valuable in-class time drilling students on standardized exam questions. Teachers recognize test preparation as necessary in this era of high-stakes standardized exams, but most can't afford to spend precious class time on test preparation activities. Instead, they can use collaborative online learning platforms to facilitate test practice for students. Doing so provides a space for them to work together to develop stronger test-taking strategies and skills.

7. Facilitate Group Work That Works

Any teacher who has facilitated a group work assignment in class knows the frustration of time wasted. Online collaborative group work gives students the flexibility to participate asynchronously when they have time, and it eliminates wasted time in class. Technology also creates transparency because it is easier to see who has done what, making the work online more equitable.

8. Communicate More Effectively With All Students

Many learning platforms have built-in message systems that make it possible for teachers to communicate with individual students or groups of students easily. Teachers can make announcements, amend assignments, change due dates, and address questions using the message option—without having to wait until the next school day.

Teachers who are inclined can also arrange virtual office hours using Skype, Google+ Hangout, or other real-time chat tools to support students outside the classroom.

9. Build Community and Relationships

Teachers can use the online space to build student relationships. Online icebreakers are a great way to get students talking, using each other's names and practicing online etiquette. These fun informal conversations translate into a stronger in-class community. This is one of the blended learning benefits that I personally have experienced, much to my satisfaction and delight. Chapter 5 introduces a variety of online icebreakers that are compatible with online learning platforms.

10. Have Fun

The Internet gives teachers access to more information than ever before. Most learning platforms allow teachers to embed pictures, videos, PDFs, and other documents, making it easy to take the best online resources and present them in the safe space of your online learning platform.

Discussions Are Critical to a Successful Blended Learning Model

My belief that discussions play a vital role in the learning process is well grounded and shared by leading experts in the academic community. Discussion becomes even more important when students are working remotely for any portion of their learning. Students who complete work at home via computer can be extremely isolated; however, the online space provides many opportunities for students to connect and talk. Learning to capitalize on the social nature of students using social media and online discussion tools is critical to maximizing the effectiveness of a blended learning model. To be superior or comparable to the traditional teaching model, blended learning must engage students and provide interactions that exceed those possible in the physical classroom.

In *The Importance of Conversation in Learning and the Value of Web-Based Discussion Tools,* Heidi Elmendorf and John Ottenhoff (2009) stress the importance of discussion as an essential part of the learning process:

> We know, usually on an intuitive level, how social dialogue can allow students to explore the shape of knowledge and its construction, ask questions and experiment with answers, and build complexity from a broadened foundation of perspectives contributed by their peers. (para. 4)

The act of telling or explaining what they know cements students' understanding of concepts. Conversely, students who are struggling benefit from hearing their peers' ideas, opinions, and explanations. Even the opportunity to ask questions can help students begin to deconstruct challenging ideas or concepts.

The old adage that "there is no such thing as a dumb question" applies absolutely. Hammering home the idea that all questions are welcomed and encouraged will make students less reticent about asking for clarification on points they do not understand. Doing so in a safe Internet space, where they don't have to worry about negative nonverbal cues or fear feeling foolish in front of a whole class, makes it even easier.

I wholeheartedly believe that the potential of the group far exceeds the intellect of any one individual in the classroom—myself included. Despite my passionate belief that discussions are an integral part of the learning process, I repeatedly failed at generating successful discussions in class. The same four or five students dominated discussions, while the rest of the class sunk low in their chairs, avoiding eye contact.

Even though most teachers believe in the value of discussion, it is often neglected in the classroom. There are a variety of impediments to real-time discussions that exclude the majority of students from participating. This lack of equity in face-to-face discussions creates an imbalance that can be corrected when discussions take place asynchronously online. This asynchronous environment provides something in-class discussion can't: *time.*

Most students need time to process information before responding to a question. Yet in traditional classrooms, time is a luxury most teachers do not have. With pressure to close the achievement gap, differentiate instruction, raise test scores, and prepare kids for college, discussions seem extravagant and time consuming.

In "Effective Classroom Discussions," Selma Wassermann (2010) describes the common teacher experience:

> So much to be done! So little time! The pressure on teachers to get everything done by the end of the school day is formidable. That race with the clock often forces teachers to speed up lessons and makes them lose patience with students who need more time to say what's on their minds. (para. 9)

Wassermann identifies a key conflict in the classroom: the race against the clock to cover curriculum versus the desire to give students a voice in class discussions. She accurately depicts the frustration, impatience, and fear that many teachers face when attempting to incorporate dynamic discussions into their classrooms.

When teachers introduce an online avenue where students are able to express their thoughts outside the time crunch of a normal school day, all students are given the equal opportunity to have a voice in the class. This equity of voice fosters relationship building, increases participation, and encourages deeper engagement with the subject area content.

Many students do not feel confident in their understanding of the curricula and hesitate to contribute to a conversation about the subject matter. Students tend to "perceive their role in the course as limited to obtaining (memorizing) information, rather than also using this information," Elmendorf and Ottenhoff (2009, para. 7) note. Transitioning students into the role of discussion leaders, facilitators, or, at the very least, active contributors begins to shift this antiquated perception of the student's role in the classroom.

When students begin redefining their role in a class from passive observer to active participant, they also begin to recognize each other as valuable resources and understand that teachers are not the only source of wisdom and "correct answers."

The quick pace of a real-time discussion, usually dominated by the vocal few, makes engaging in the conversation challenging. Students who are shy or anxious recede into the background under the stress of in-class conversations. Online discussion boards encourage "independent learning and critical thinking skills, and provide a comfortable environment for students who are reluctant to speak in class. Shy and timid students are more likely to participate and ask questions online than they might be in class" (Lyons, 2004, para. 9). This creates equity of voice that makes it possible for every member of the class to be involved. The intellectual benefits combined with the relationship building that blossoms with the use of online discussions translate into more successful in-class conversations and stronger classroom community.

Another barrier to participation in real-time conversations in the classroom is the desire to record important information and ideas shared during a discussion. As Wassermann (2010) states, in-class discussions are typically rapid and ephemeral—to the point that students have two choices: either participate and have the conversation quickly fade from memory or abstain to take notes and capture the conversation for future reference. During an online discussion, students can actively participate without worrying about taking notes because there is an electronic transcript of the conversation that can be easily accessed for future reference after the discussion is over.

The benefits of engaging all students in the class dialogue, providing time needed to process and respond, while creating an online transcript of the work done make online discussions an attractive addition to the work done in class. In addition to these practical benefits, discussion skills are essential to life. In particular, online communication and collaboration skills are rapidly becoming essential 21st century skills.

In *The Use of Discussion and Questioning in the Classroom*, Brandi Davidson (2007) states,

> Students need to know how to participate in meaningful discussion. This is an invaluable skill that will be used throughout their academic career, as well as in the work force. When students are involved in meaningful discussions, they learn from each other and are encouraged to think critically about and explore thoroughly what they are learning. (para. 2)

Learning to communicate via a variety of mediums will allow students to be successful in the years that follow high school. As teachers we must incorporate this technology into our teaching methodology to adequately prepare our students for a smooth transition into higher education and the workforce.

Community-of-Inquiry Framework

Community of inquiry literally refers to a group of individuals who share a common interest or physical space and engage in a question-driven search for truth or knowledge. An educational community of inquiry is defined as "a group of individuals who collaboratively engage in purposeful critical discourse and reflection to construct personal meaning and confirm mutual understanding" (*COI Model*, n.d., para. 1). This search for understanding via "purposeful critical discourse" can be challenging to achieve in the physical classroom given the variety of barriers that impede student participation.

Researchers such as D. R. Garrison have explored the way an online environment can be used to facilitate discussions and collaborative work to create a community of inquiry and engage students in deep and meaningful learning.

There are three interrelated components of the community-of-inquiry framework: social presence, teaching presence, and cognitive presence.

Social Presence

Social presence is the student's ability to "establish personal and purposeful relationships" (Garrison, 2007, p. 63) through open and effective communication. The development of an individual's social presence in an online environment makes it possible for him or her to form meaningful relationships with other members of the online community. These relationships are fundamental to the long-term success of students' interactions and the quality of their learning. This is why it is so important for teachers to begin online work by clearly establishing their expectations for participation and fostering the development of respectful and supportive relationships. Chapter 5 presents strategies and provides resources to support the development of students' social presence online.

Teaching Presence

Teaching presence is the combination of direct instruction, curriculum design, and online facilitation, all of which are discussed throughout this text. Direct instruction in the Teacher-Designed Blend is the time spent in the physical classroom directing and supporting learning. The student-centered in-class activities described in Chapters 6–9 provide a variety of lesson ideas for teachers who want to use their direct instruction to place students at the center of the learning process.

Traditionally, teachers stand at the front of the room disseminating information while students are the receivers of that information. The goal of this book is to support teachers in using technology to create more opportunities for students to be active participants in their learning.

The image below reflects the flow of information in the traditional teaching paradigm. Information flows from teacher to student and, at times, from student to teacher.

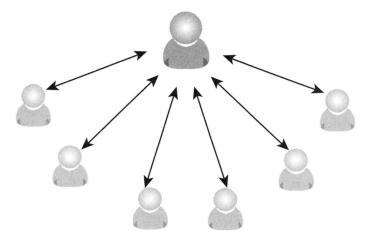

However, in a community of inquiry the flow of ideas and information must also move from student to student, as seen in the visual below.

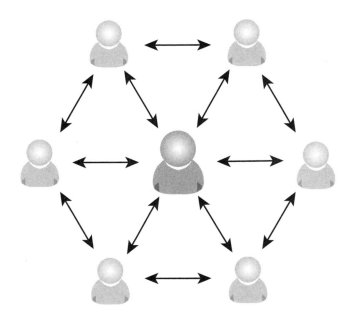

Curriculum design is discussed in Chapter 4, which explores strategies for designing strong questions that will drive dynamic discussions. Chapters 6–9 each focus on a specific subject—English, history/social studies, science, and math—and provide examples of online discussion questions and tasks to show educators how an online environment can be used to engage students, inspire higher-order thinking, and address the Common Core State Standards.

Facilitation styles are discussed in Chapter 3. A teacher's student population and learning objectives will ultimately dictate which facilitation style that teacher chooses for his or her work online.

Cognitive Presence

Garrison (2007) defines cognitive presence "as the exploration, construction, resolution and confirmation of understanding through collaboration and reflection" (p. 65). Students must move beyond simply forming relationships to working together and communicating effectively to explore information, ask questions, and come to resolutions. For students to be successful in an academic inquiry, they must have a strong social presence, and teachers must clearly outline the expectations for work done online. Students must also share a common purpose or goal to develop the cognitive presence.

Together, social presence, teaching presence, and cognitive presence create an online community capable of engaging students in collaborative learning that shifts the paradigm from a teacher-centered to a student-centered model.

Chapter Summary

The term *blended learning* refers to a spectrum of teaching modes that combine traditional face-to-face instruction with work done online. Many teachers fear that adopting a blended learning approach will devalue their role, result in less face time with students, and diminish their control over the design and delivery of curriculum.

I advocate for teachers to claim the term *blended learning*. I believe it gives them a voice in the way technology is integrated into their traditional curriculum. The resources available online have made this an exciting time to be a teacher. The trick is learning how to adopt and integrate online tools that will work for us.

This book focuses on an emerging blended learning model I call the Teacher-Designed Blend. In this model the teacher drives the integration of technology and uses it to complement existing curriculum to improve learning outcomes for students and create student-centered classrooms.

The community-of-inquiry framework provides a guide for the successful development of an online educational community. The community of inquiry is composed of three interdependent elements: social presence, teaching presence, and cognitive presence. Together, these components have the potential to engage students in meaningful conversations and cooperative collaboration that places students in the center of the learning process.

Book Study Questions

1. How might you approach a blended learning model given your curriculum? Are there activities you do in class that you can imagine moving online? If so, describe them. What work might be more successful online than in the classroom? How would using the online space create more time and flexibility in your classroom?

2. What fears do you have about the blended approach to instruction? How might you address these fears when blending online work with the work done in class?

3. How would you expect your students and their parents to react to this type of blended instruction? Would your administrators support your attempts to integrate an online component to complement your in-class work? How would you articulate your decision to embrace a blended learning approach to skeptical students, parents, and/or administrators?

4. What online resources or tools do you currently use with your students? Why do you use these? Do they save you time? If so, how? How do they positively benefit your teaching and/or your students' learning? How did you find out about these resources or tools?

5. What benefits would you expect to experience by adopting a blended learning model? How might it positively impact your teaching and/or your students' learning? What pain points associated with teaching might be mitigated by using a blended approach to instruction?

6. What are discussions currently like in your classroom? What barriers exist that make it challenging to engage all students in conversations? What strategies do you currently employ to motivate students to contribute to in-class discussions?

7. How might taking discussions online make them more successful? What factors might cause a student to engage in an online discussion versus an in-class discussion? What challenges do you think you might encounter taking conversations online?

8. What skills do you use in your daily life and in your work that you consider critical to your success? Brainstorm a list of the top 10 skills you believe to be most important to your success in life. How did you develop these skills? How do you teach these skills?

9. Are you currently teaching digital literacy—the ability to locate, organize, understand, evaluate, and analyze information using digital technology—in your curriculum? If so, how? How will digital literacy support student success beyond your classroom and subject area?

10. How might integrating an online education platform provide you with the time and flexibility to shift to a more student-centered classroom? What would a student-centered classroom look like in your subject area? What skills would students develop if your classroom were student-centered as opposed to teacher-centered? What benefits and/or drawbacks would you anticipate in a student-centered classroom? How might shifting to a student-centered classroom require you to grow and develop as an educator?

References

CDW. (2011). *2011 CDW-G 21st-century classroom report.* Available from http://newsroom.cdw.com/features/feature-06-27-11.html

COI model. (2011). Retrieved from http://communitiesofinquiry.com/model

Davidson, B. (2007). *The use of discussion and questioning in the classroom.* http://www.associatedcontent.com/article/243147/the_use_of_discussion_and_questioning.html

Elmendorf, H., & Ottenhoff, J. (2009). *The Importance of conversation in learning and the value of Web-based discussion tools.* Retrieved from http://www.academiccommons.org/commons/essay/importance-conversation-learning

Garrison, D. R. (2007). Online community of inquiry review: Social, cognitive, and teaching presence issues. *Journal of Asynchronous Learning Networks, 11*(1), 61–72.

Herrera, L. (2011, January 17). In Florida, virtual classrooms with no teachers. *New York Times*, p. A15. Retrieved from http://www.nytimes.com

Horn, M. B., & Staker, H. (n.d.). *The rise of k–12 blended learning.* Retrieved from http://www.innosightinstitute.org/innosight/wp-content/uploads/2011/01/The-Rise-of-K-12-Blended-Learning.pdf

Lyons, J. F. (2004). Teaching U.S. history online: Problems and prospects. *The History Teacher, 37*(4). Retrieved from http://www.historycooperative.org/htindex.html

Wassermann, S. (2010). Effective classroom discussions. *Educational Leadership, 67*(5). Retrieved from http://www.ascd.org/publications/educational-leadership.aspx

3

The Role of the Teacher in a Blended Learning Model

This chapter focuses on the teaching presence, which is the "design, facilitation, and direction of cognitive and social processes for the purpose of realizing personally meaningful and educationally worthwhile learning outcomes" (Akyol 2011). Designing, facilitating, and directing student work online requires a slightly different skill set than that of the traditional teacher in the classroom.

Teaching students how to communicate, collaborate, ask questions, and problem solve is easier to do in the context of the physical classroom for most teachers who are technology immigrants. However, it is critical to develop an online community to complement your in-class work to ensure students are actively engaging with their peers in meaningful conversations. These online discussions must build what Garrison (2007) describes as "personal and purposeful relationships" (p. 63) and support student progression from "exploration to resolution" (p. 61).

Given that student-centered learning and the community-of-inquiry framework are both based on constructivist theories, they both value many of the same principles and can be used in conjunction to ensure that the blended learning model supports teachers in using their work online to more effectively transition to a student-centered classroom.

Choosing a Learning Platform or Learning Management System

Choosing the right learning platform or learning management system for your individual needs is critical to adopting a blended learning model that will work for you and your students in the long term. For clarification purposes, it is important to note that a learning platform is an interactive online space that provides teachers and students with information and resources to improve the delivery and management of curriculum. In contrast, a learning management system (LMS) is a larger-scale software application that helps teachers administer, track, report, and document student progress online. The ideas in this book can be applied using a variety of learning platforms and LMSs.

Identifying your needs is a necessary first step in finding the right tool. Here is a list of questions to consider:

- What will the primary purpose of your learning platform or LMS be?
- Do you plan to support an entirely online course, or are you teaching a blended instruction course?
- Do you want to support discussions? Post assignments? Foster group work outside of class? Make grades available online?
- Do you plan to incorporate multimedia into your site? If so, what kinds of media?
- Do you want your site to be an academic one, or will you allow students to use it informally to have conversations about topics that are not related to the curriculum?
- Do you already have a Web space on your school site that administration wants you to use to post homework? If not, do you want a learning platform or LMS where you can post homework assignments and announcements?
- Do you want to give online quizzes and tests via your site?
- Do you want your site to collect data on your students' participation and/or performance via a reporting system?
- Does your school require an online grade book? If so, has the district provided a free grade book? If so, are you required to use that one, or do you have the freedom to choose one on your own?

- What are the biggest hurdles to student access to technology at your school? How can you ensure all students have a way to access your site? Are there computer labs on campus? Is there a school library (or nearby public library) with computers available?
- Is there a district filter, which might limit your ability to use particular learning platforms and/or media?
- How much are you willing to pay to use a learning platform?

Once you have answered these questions and brainstormed any additional questions you may have, you are ready to "window shop" for the right learning platform. Several online learning platforms and LMSs allow you to take a test drive with their product if they are not already free for teachers. I highly suggest trying out your top choices before making a final decision. Ease of usability is hard to judge before you have actually experimented with a learning platform or LMS. The small nuances of color, language, and design can have a big impact when you are working with a tool daily, so you want to make sure it is just right for you.

Before getting into specific pedagogy and application, I want to review just a few of the many online learning platforms available to teachers. I choose to focus on five in particular because they support online discussions, which are a central component of the blended learning model I discuss in this book. This book does not attempt to cover all learning platforms or LMSs because there are so many currently available.

Blackboard

Blackboard is a complete LMS that can be used to support an entirely online course or a blended learning course. A white paper authored by David Yaskin and Dr. Deborah Everhart (2002), Blackboard's vice president of product management and chief architect, respectively, states,

> The Blackboard Learning System is a web-based software system that offers industry leading course management, Building Blocks Architecture for customization and interoperability, and a scalable, modular design that allows for integration with K–12 student information systems, third-party instructional applications, authentication schema, and security protocols. (p. 3)

Moodle

Moodle, an acronym for Modular Object-Oriented Dynamic Learning Environment, describes itself as "a software package for producing Internet-based courses and web sites" (*About Moodle*, 2012, para. 3). It is built on an activity-based model that combines activities into sequences and groups, which can help you guide participants through learning paths. Many different aspects of Moodle can be customized and personalized to fit individual instructors' needs. "Moodle functions much like the privately owned Blackboard, but because its software is open source, Moodle services are free, available to everyone and compatible with numerous program add-ons" (Herts, 2009, para. 2). Like Blackboard, Moodle can be used to support both online courses and blended learning models.

Edmodo

Edmodo is a free online "social learning platform" that provides teachers and students with a "secure place to connect and collaborate, share content and educational applications, and access homework, grades, class discussions and notifications" (Edmodo, 2012, para. 1). Edmodo says its goal is to "help educators harness the power of social media to customize the classroom" for every student (para. 1). Teachers can connect with other educators, share curriculum, and collaborate online.

Schoology

Schoology (2010) has combined social networking with learning management to create an interface for educators and students that looks and feels like Facebook. Schoology describes itself as "a cloud-based learning management system and configurable social network. . . . Schoology leverages the familiarity of popular social media tools to improve communication and collaboration" (paras. 2–3).

Collaborize Classroom

Collaborize Classroom is designed to complement classroom instruction and engage students in online activities, assignments, and discussions with the goal of increasing participation inside and outside the classroom. Collaborize Classroom prioritizes discussions and student collaboration instead of disseminating and storing information. The discussions are the central focus of the work done online.

I wanted an intuitive learning platform that would be easy for my students to navigate, while supporting dynamic discussions that would support my inquiry-based instruction. For me, Collaborize Classroom has provided an intuitive space that is simple to use, yet offers endless possibilities. I have a Web space and grade program that my school requires me to use, so I did not need many of the additional features offered by other online tools. Teachers who do not have a website or grading program offered to them by their schools may need a more complete learning platform or LMS.

The table on the following page lists the main features of each platform; however, these platforms rapidly evolve so there may be items that could be added to this chart. This is meant to give the reader an overview of the features offered by each learning platform or LMS, but it does not attempt to include every feature for each platform.

Defining Your Role as Facilitator

Once you have decided on a learning platform, it is time to define your facilitation role. Many teachers fear that adopting an online learning platform will increase instead of decrease their workload. The trick is to use online work to replace and improve what you already do.

For me, online discussions, activities, and group work have completely taken the place of the pen-and-paper worksheets, questions, and activities I assigned in the past to gauge comprehension and drive higher-order thinking.

As the teacher and facilitator of your online learning platform, you must define your role and then make that role transparent for your students. Regardless of your facilitation style, it is important that your students know you do not live online. There will be times when they post a question, and you will not respond until the next day or the next class. They may encounter technical problems that they need to troubleshoot on their own or wait to discuss with you the next school day. They cannot, and should not, expect to have access to you at all times.

Keeping your role realistic is important to ensure that your students' work online does save you time. Keep in mind that establishing an online community takes time, and learning to be an effective facilitator takes practice, but the learning curve is relatively short and the payoff is well worth the time investment.

Blackboard	Moodle	Edmodo	Schoology	Collaborize Classroom
• Announcements	• Announcements	• Announcements	• Assignments	• Structured discussions
• Assignments	• Instant messages	• Discussions	• Attendance	• Multiple question types
• Real-time chat	• Discussions	• Grade book	• Test and quiz creation	• Results page
• Discussions	• Assignment submission	• Calendar	• Grade book	• Participation reports
• Mail	• Calendar	• Quiz builder	• Calendar	• Messaging
• Course content	• File downloads	• Assignment submission	• Analytics	• Store and share content in Topic Library
• Calendar	• Grading	• Analytics	• Class profiles	• Mobile capabilities
• Learning modules	• Online quiz	• Store and share content	• Online dropbox	
• Assessments	• Wiki	• Mobile capabilities	• Messaging	
• Grade book			• Mobile capabilities	
• Media library				
• Mobile capabilities				

Here are a few questions you should consider before deciding on your role:

- How many students are you working with?
- What age level are you teaching?
- How much support do your students need when working?
- What is the goal of your online discussions?
- Will online discussions be done in class, at home, or both?

You need to select the role that best fits your needs and the needs of your students.

Silent Facilitator vs. Involved Facilitator

You can choose to be a silent facilitator, an involved facilitator, or a combination of the two, depending on your student population and your objectives. There are benefits to each style of facilitation. It is important that you articulate a clear role for your involvement in the online environment so students know what to expect during online discussions and work.

Silent Facilitator

A teacher who uses online discussions and work to complement and extend in-class curriculum may choose to be a silent facilitator who limits his or her involvement to posting questions for students to discuss and designing activities for students to complete. This role gives students the opportunity to take charge of the discussion and, subsequently, their own discovery of knowledge.

Teachers who choose not to engage actively in the discussions should take the information, insights, questions, and ideas presented in the online space and weave them back into the classroom. Even though you are not actively participating in the discussions taking place online, this lets your students know that you are monitoring the discussions and using them to drive work that is done in the classroom.

By restricting the teacher role to that of a silent facilitator, the teacher does not filter the information or determine the direction of the discussion. Instead, students are allowed to engage freely in dialogue with their peers, steering the course of the conversation to make it more meaningful.

A silent facilitator must be willing to "let go" and relinquish control. Discussions may not go where you anticipated. This can be a challenge for a type-A teacher (like me), but the reward is seeing a discussion blossom without your involvement. I have had several moments when I was floored by the quality of responses, thoughtful replies to peers, and insightful questions. I have come to realize that at times my involvement in discussions has probably stifled my students' creativity.

Involved Facilitator

A teacher working with younger students, a smaller group of students, or a group that needs more support may choose to be an involved facilitator, regularly engaging in the discussion. This role allows the teacher to steer the direction of the dialogue to ensure that conversations stay focused on particular aspects of the curriculum. The teacher also has the opportunity to model online etiquette, ask follow-up questions, compliment student responses, and clarify confusion online.

The teacher who chooses to be an involved facilitator must be careful not to dominate the discussion or post an overwhelming number of responses or replies. Again, it's important to decide on a degree of involvement that is realistic and then make that clear to students. It can be helpful for an involved facilitator to limit his or her responses to the same number of responses required of a single student in the class. This alleviates the burden of feeling that the facilitator must respond to each student or each discussion topic.

Involved facilitators must walk a fine line with their involvement because they do not want to overpower conversations. It is important to limit commentary and allow students to reach their own conclusions, even if it takes time. Teachers involved in the conversation must also avoid becoming the source of all "right answers" as this limits the potential of the group.

The quality of your feedback as an involved participant is also critical to the success of your role as facilitator. Keeping feedback specific, genuine, and authentic is key to maintaining credibility with students. Avoid vague, generic, or repetitive positive feedback. This is another reason that limiting responses is important. If you feel you must give all students equal quality feedback, then your online discussions will create more work for you.

Fluctuating between the two roles can also work. For example, I have chosen to be a silent facilitator for 90% of our online discussions. I prefer to allow my students to explore topics and direct the course of a discussion or debate—partly because I know if I get involved it would be next to impossible to limit my commentary. That said, I use my Collaborize Classroom site for peer editing during essay writing.

I ask students to post parts of an essay draft (e.g., introduction paragraph with thesis statement, best example of quote introduction) for peer feedback. Then I provide individual feedback as needed to correct errors, suggest improvements, and compliment strong writing. During their writing process, I am able to provide feedback to students that is more timely than collecting dozens of papers, writing feedback on them, and passing them back.

Students also benefit from seeing the feedback their peers receive. If one student received a note to revise an aspect of his or her writing, that student can reference writing posted by a peer that received praise to see what a stronger piece of writing looks like. This embedded modeling can help support students who are struggling. Traditionally, when students get feedback, they are the only ones who see and benefit from that feedback.

In my experience teaching professional development courses, many teachers have said they plan to begin their work as an involved participant to establish norms, reinforce expectations, and motivate quality discussions with questions, compliments, and suggestions. Then they plan to recede into the background, becoming silent facilitators, as students become proficient participants in the online space.

Determining your role will depend on your learning objectives, your student population, and, ultimately, your personality type. Choose the role that you are most comfortable with, communicate that role to your students, and make sure you set realistic expectations for yourself.

	Silent Facilitator	*Involved Participant*
Individual Responsibilities	• Communicate with students via individual messages, via e-mail, or in person to compliment strong contributions or encourage development of online work. • Respond to student questions and concerns via individual messages, via e-mail, or in person.	• Respond to strong postings with complimentary feedback, ask follow-up questions to redirect the conversation, encourage more depth in student responses, play devil's advocate, offer insights, make connections, clarify confusions, etc.

	Silent Facilitator	Involved Participant
	• Design student-centered in-class activities that build on the work done in the online space, and effectively weave the two learning environments together.	• Use any safe space violations as teachable moments in the actual conversation. • Answer student questions in the online forum so all students can benefit from the answer.
Shared Responsibilities	• Post questions to drive higher-order thinking and engage students in dynamic discussions. • Read student responses in a timely manner to ensure the tone of the conversation stays respectful. • Remove any postings that are not conducive to maintaining a safe space online. • Actively refer to and draw from online discussions while in class to ensure students see the value of their discussion in relation to the curriculum. • Use participation reports to assess participation in the online discussion according to set expectations.	

Effectively Differentiate Instruction With Online Discussions

Teachers using an online learning platform or LMS will find it is significantly easier to design learning opportunities that are customized using media, question design, and grouping strategies to meet the needs of a diverse student population.

Differentiation is a hot topic in education. Differentiated instruction "is the practice of modifying and adapting instruction, materials, content, student projects and products, and assessment to meet the learning needs of individual students" (Logsdon, 2011, para. 1). As class sizes grow exponentially, teachers face the daunting task of teaching an increasingly wide range of students with various abilities, learning styles, accommodations, and levels of proficiency in a single class. Teachers must stimulate and engage intellectually gifted students while scaffolding curriculum to support struggling students and/or second language learners. This delicate balance is what many argue separates the best teachers from the herd.

Differentiated instruction involves assessing student knowledge in a given content area, then using a variety of strategies to create effective curriculum that is, in effect, individualized. Designing curriculum of varied complexity, using different grouping strategies, modifying outcomes and product expectations, tailoring delivery, and providing tiered projects are all critical elements in differentiating instruction.

Differentiated instruction excites the brilliant student to uncover deeper layers of learning while simultaneously structuring curriculum to support lower-level students or students with learning disabilities—both identified and unidentified.

I read an interesting blog post titled "21 Things That Will Become Obsolete in Education by 2020," by Shelley Blake-Plock (2011). He argues,

> The 21st century is customizable. In ten years, the teacher who hasn't yet figured out how to use technology to personalize learning will be the teacher out of a job. Differentiation won't make you "distinguished"; it'll just be a natural part of your work. (para. 6)

Blake-Plock makes a valid argument that differentiation is a necessary skill that effective teachers need to teach individual students. The role technology will play in making this individualized curriculum manageable for teachers is exciting, but it will require that teachers, especially those in credential school, learn how to effectively use the technology available to them.

Online learning platforms and LMSs can support a variety of groups—student pairs, performance based, self-selected, random, preferred learning style. Online learning teams and group work allow teachers to assemble students by skill level, interest, or preferred learning style to achieve desired learning outcomes.

Pairing students to allow for peer teaching is another method of reinforcing the strong student's understanding of material while providing a struggling student with a peer instructor. This reciprocal learning style is another way teachers can use the strengths in their classrooms to create differentiated instruction.

For example, I used my Collaborize Classroom site to create online character focus groups during *The Joy Luck Club* unit to help students better understand the characters in the Amy Tan's novel. The story focuses on four mother-daughter pairs, and each character tells two stories. Students find it challenging to keep the mothers, daughters, and secondary characters straight while reading.

To support students in their comprehension of the novel, I divided the class into mother–daughter focus groups. I designed the groups so there was a balance of stronger students with lower-level students. The stronger students in each team focused on the mother's story, while the students who tended to struggle focused on the daughter's stories. The mother's stories, which take place in China, are more challenging; the daughter's stories, which take place in the United States, are less complex. Each night for homework students engaged in online discussions about their characters, which provided them with a much deeper understanding of the novel and created a support network of peers who could answer questions and provide clarification.

This structure made it possible for me to challenge my most capable students while supporting my lower-level students. The mother–daughter focus groups also allowed students in each group to ask questions, discuss events, and share thoughts on their characters. It created a mini learning community within our larger class to support students in their comprehension and analysis of the novel.

Just as consumers know that a one-size-fits-all approach does not work when buying a pair of jeans, educators know that one standard approach to teaching will not meet the needs of all—or even most—students. Without an attempt to vary instruction to meet the specific needs of individual students, the curriculum is bound to bore some and baffle others. Differentiating instruction is the key to reaching all students.

In addition to grouping strategies, teachers can use media to differentiate instruction. When students are able to read an article, analyze a complex graph, or watch a video at their own pace at home, they are able to think deeply about the nuances of the information presented. The rapid pace of classwork makes it challenging for students who have language barriers, have learning disabilities, or just need more time to process to be successful. Embedding media into a discussion question or online topic puts students in control of the play button. For example, if a teacher has embedded a video into the class's online space, the stronger students can watch it once and work quickly. In contrast, a student who is struggling may want to pause the video or watch it several times to fully understand the information presented.

The flexibility provided by an online learning platform or LMS allows differentiated instruction to transcend the 60- or 90-minute class period. Teachers can design activities, projects, research tasks, and creative assignments that extend beyond the physical classroom to support students at various levels.

This practice of varying curriculum to meet the needs of a diverse population of students is increasingly challenging as student populations increase and an ever-greater number of programs are cut; however, technology has the potential to lighten the load for teachers.

Weaving Online Work Back Into the Classroom

Using work online to complement traditional in-class instruction is most effective if teachers are able to weave the two mediums together. They should not be viewed as two separate and disconnected arenas of learning, but rather as interlacing modes of instruction. By combining the various elements of in-class instruction with conversations and activities taking place in the online learning platform, the inter-connectedness of ideas will result in higher comprehension and lasting retention of information.

I continually weave our online conversations and work back into the classroom. This is one reason I chose Collaborize Classroom; it has a "publish to results" option that takes the outcomes of a conversation and creates a chart to show the breakdown of choices, ideas, and viewpoints. This makes it easy for me to draw that tangible outcome back into the class for follow-up discussions, debates, and activities.

The following are examples of information flows to support teachers in effectively weaving their work in the online space back into the physical classroom. In these flowcharts, the light gray boxes denote what happens in the classroom, while the dark gray boxes refer to online work.

1. Online Discussions

2. Notes and Assignments Posted Online

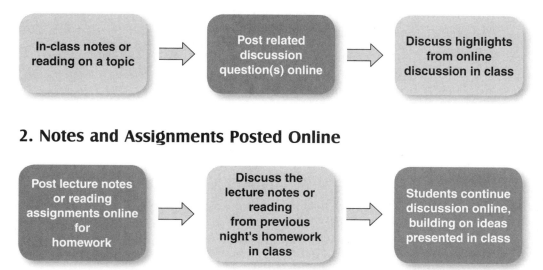

3. Collaborative Group Work

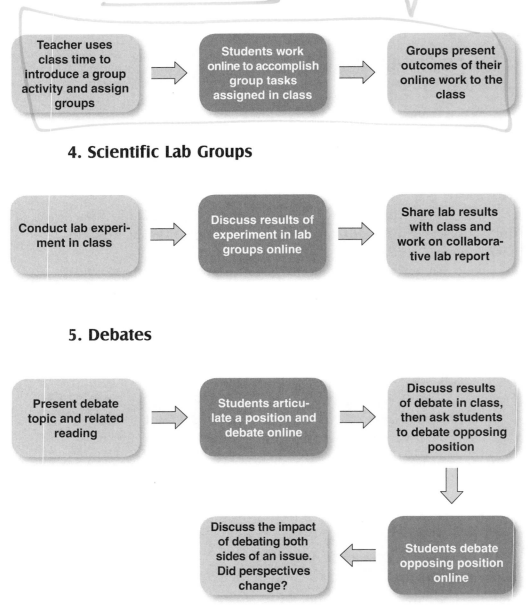

4. Scientific Lab Groups

5. Debates

Chapter Summary

The teaching presence is the element in the community-of-inquiry framework that focuses on design, facilitation, and direct instruction. To create a blended learning model, instructors must decide on a learning platform or learning management system that will best meet their needs. Facilitating the work completed online requires that teachers identify the best facilitation role for their student population, then make that role transparent so students know what to expect when working online.

Individualizing and personalizing instruction is important, and it is made easier in the online space where students can work at their own pace. Teachers can use grouping strategies and media to further differentiate instruction. Finally, teachers must actively weave together the work done online with the work done in class to maximize the value of the work done in each space—physical and virtual.

Book Study Questions

1. What are the primary objectives of your online work? What do you hope to accomplish by engaging students online? Do you think you will need a learning platform or a comprehensive learning management system (LMS)?

2. Have you explored any of the learning platforms or LMSs available online? If so, which ones? What did you like and/or dislike about them? If not, what features do you want and/or need in a learning platform or LMS?

3. Which facilitation style—silent or involved facilitator—do you think will be the best fit for you and your students? Why? What advantages does this facilitation style have that you find appealing? Do you anticipate any challenges with this facilitation style?

4. Do you have any fears about facilitation? If so, how will you address these fears? What strategies will you use to ensure that your work online saves you time rather than adding to your workload?

5. What strategies do you currently use to differentiate and personalize instruction in your classroom? Can you adapt any of these strategies for the online space? How diverse is your student population? What special needs do your students have? How will you use grouping strategies, question design, and/or media to more effectively differentiate your instruction online?

6. How will weaving together online work with in-class work improve learning outcomes for your students? What might be challenging about weaving online work into the physical classroom? What strategies might you use to do this more effectively?

References

About Moodle: Pedagogy. (2012). Retrieved from http://docs.moodle.org/19/en/Talk:About_Moodle

Akyol, Z. (2011) *Coi model.* Community of Inquiry. Retrieved from http://communitiesofinquiry.com/model

Blake-Plock, S. (2011). *21 things that will become obsolete in education by 2020.* Retrieved from http://dcamd.com/2011/01/28/21-things-that-will-become-obsolete-in-education-by-2020

Edmodo. (2012). *About.* Retrieved from http://about.edmodo.com/?subdomain=www

Garrison, D. R. (2007). Online community of inquiry review: Social, cognitive, and teaching presence issues. *Journal of Asynchronous Learning Networks, 11*(1), 61–72.

Herts, J. (2009, April 22). Vassar to switch from Blackboard to Moodle. *Miscellany News.* Retrieved from http://www.miscellanynews.com/2.1576/vassar-to-switch-from-blackboard-to-moodle-1.1728215#

Logsdon, A. (2011). *Differentiated instruction—Meet student needs with differentiated instruction.* Retrieved from http://learningdisabilities.about.com/od/df/g/differentiated.htm

Schoology. (2010). *Schoology secures $1.25 million Series A funding.* Retrieved from http://blog.schoology.com/2010/06/schoology-secures-1-25-million-series-a-funding/

Yaskin, D., & Everhart, D. (2002). *K–12 solutions: Product overview.* Washington, DC: Blackboard. Retrieved from http://library.blackboard.com/docs/k12/Bb_Whitepaper_K12_Learning_System.pdf

4

The Art of Asking
Questions Online

Internet Workshop

Designing quality questions is the primary role of a teacher facilitating online work and discussions. Strong questions help lead students to a deeper understanding of the curriculum. Asking the "right" question that will drive a dynamic conversation is an art form. It is crucial that a facilitator formulate questions that do the following:

- Excite curiosity
- Engage higher-level thinking skills: analysis, synthesis, evaluation, and creation
- Encourage multiple points of view
- Challenge thought, not stifle it
- Fortify understanding of curriculum
- Inspire the application of knowledge in new and innovative ways
- Draw on personal experiences and perspectives
- Foster collaboration
- Build a strong community
- Model strategies for formulating quality questions
- Teach students how to ask their own questions

Encourage Conversations With Well-Chosen Questions

Some question types, such as the following, foster conversations, while others kill conversations before they start.

- Why?
- How?
- What?
- Would?
- Could?
- Should?
- What if?

Question Types That Foster Conversation

The following are question types that lead to more successful conversations online.

Subjective Questions

Subjective questions require students to produce information based on personal opinion. Each answer varies based on the subjective point of view being presented. The person or group of people being asked the question must make sense of the subject at hand using their individual perspectives. This type of question encourages students to explain the *how* or *why* using examples and facts from their lives to support their statements.

Evaluative Questions

Evaluative questions have no wrong answer because they ask students to evaluate information and formulate a response based on their opinions and beliefs. Because students enter the classroom (traditional or online) with their own lifetime of experiences that color their opinions and perspectives, these questions invite a more personal dialogue. Evaluating an issue, topic, piece of information, or situation allows students to assess the quality, significance, and value of the topic at hand, using their particular viewpoints to support those judgments.

Problem-Solving Questions

Problem-solving questions present a situation, dilemma, challenge, or problem to be solved. Students approach problem solving in a variety of ways, which leads to rich conversations about strategies, rationales, and unforeseen obstacles.

Brainstorming Questions

Brainstorming questions ask students to generate a large number of ideas. The quantity and diversity of ideas is crucial to the success of brainstorming questions, which effectively encourages a variety of responses. When engaging students in a brainstorming activity, remind them not to edit their responses. The goal is to generate a large number of ideas. Editing their answers will limit their creativity.

Debate Questions

Debate questions ask students to take a position on an issue, then provide a justification for their position. Students must understand the topic, provide convincing evidence, address counterarguments, and organize their points to maximize their effectiveness. Critical thinking allows debaters to find logical flaws in the analysis of their opponents' position and be able to see when an argument is not being supported. Critical thinking is the cornerstone of good debate (Scott, 2008).

Questions that ask students to take a side on an issue or topic effectively promote lively conversations between students with opposing viewpoints, while allowing students with similar viewpoints to find commonality with one another.

Consider These Sample Questions

I have designed a series of example question grids for English, history/social studies, science, and math. Each subject-specific grid has examples of each type of question discussed above (subjective, evaluative, problem solving, brainstorming, and debate) for each grade level (upper elementary school, middle school, and high school). These are intended to serve as strong examples of the types of questions that will foster dynamic discussions.

As I mentioned earlier, it is ideal if questions are layered, so educators will want to develop additional questions to complement these examples.

English Question Grid

Question Type	Upper Elementary School	Middle School	High School
Subjective	If you were given the same choice as Peak Marcello in Roland Smith's book *Peak* to either spend 3 years in a juvenile detention center or climb Mount Everest, which would you choose? Would it be more challenging to be locked up without your freedom or be forced to climb one of the highest mountains in the world? What are the pros and cons of each choice that might impact your decision?	How does Stanley in Louis Sachar's novel *Holes* develop and grow as a character during his time at Camp Green Lake? Does he change mentally or physically? Where in the book do you see him develop?	William Golding has said, "The theme of *Lord of the Flies* is an attempt to trace the defects of a society back to the defects of human nature." Do you think this is the central theme? Based on your interpretation of the novel, what are the principle defects in human nature that lead to the breakdown of the boys' ability to govern themselves and maintain order? At what point in the novel is order completely lost?
Evaluative	Which theme from Madeleine L'Engle's book *A Wrinkle in Time* do you think is most powerful? Why do you believe this central idea is so important in the book? Where do you see this theme in the book? • good vs. evil • family relationships • love • courage	In Ray Bradbury's short story "There Will Come Soft Rains," what is his main message about society? What happened to the society in this story? What is implied (hinted at) about human nature in this story?	Do you agree or disagree with the criticism of the feudal society as expressed in the subtext of "The Nun's Priest's Tale" in Chaucer's *Canterbury Tales?* What is the criticism of the feudal society in the story? Why do you think it is or is not a legitimate critique of feudal society during Chaucer's time?
Problem solving	In Lucretia Hale's book *The Peterkin Papers*, choose one unusual problem facing the Pepins, and explain how you would have solved this problem if it had	In Jack London's book *Call of the Wild*, how could Buck have escaped his captivity prior to meeting Thorton? Describe a	In section two, "The Sieve and the Sand," of Ray Bradbury's *Fahrenheit 451*, Guy Montag is faced with the dilemma of maintaining his role as a conformist or

Question Type	*Upper Elementary School*	*Middle School*	*High School*
	happened to you. These are quirky problems, so your solutions should be creative! What would you do if . . . • your piano was delivered and set in front of the living room window backward? • you woke up to find toads in your shoes? • you put salt in your drink? • your kitchen utensils started to disappear?	moment of opportunity and how you would have escaped if you were Buck.	challenging the rules that govern society to become a nonconformist. What path(s) would allow Montag to challenge conformity while protecting himself (and those he loves) from danger?
Brainstorming	Describe an average day in Peter Sis's book *The Wall: Growing Up Behind the Iron Curtain.* Brainstorm the ways life in the book is either similar to or different from your own life today.	In Wilson Rawls' book *Where the Red Fern Grows,* Billy demonstrates determination in many difficult situations. Brainstorm examples of Billy's determination in the novel.	Scout, the narrator of *To Kill a Mockingbird,* is influenced by a variety of social factors in the novel that affect her views on race and equality. Brainstorm all of the factors (major and minor) that impact her views on these topics.
Debate	In Gary Paulsen's novel *Hatchet,* Brian demonstrates patience in a variety of situations. Do you believe Brian's patience saved his life? If yes, give an example of his patience from the book. If no, what quality do you think was most important? Give an example.	In Paolo Bacigalupi's novel *Ship Breaker,* the characters debate whether it is better to be smart or lucky. If you could choose to be smart or lucky, which would you choose and why?	Do you think George made the "right" decision when he killed Lennie in the final scene of Steinbeck's novel *Of Mice and Men?* Why or why not?

History/Social Studies Question Grid

Question Type	Upper Elementary School	Middle School	High School
Subjective	How would you define "democracy" in your own words so that a 5-year-old would understand this term? Think about the vocabulary and examples you are using. Remember that children love to ask "why," so make sure you answer the whys in your explanation.	What factors do you believe led to the American Revolution? Identify three specific factors, and analyze their impact.	What do you think was the most significant human rights violation of the 20th century? Who was targeted? Who was the oppressor? How did the global community respond to this human rights violation?
Evaluative	What do you believe was the most important message or idea in Confucius's teaching? Why do you think this idea in his teaching was so significant? How did his ideas impact Chinese society, government, and/or social relationships?	Select one debate that took place at the Constitutional Convention to evaluate. What was the debate about? What were the two sides of the debate? What was the resolution? Do you think this was the best resolution?	What was the impact of the United States' decision to enter World War I? What was the United States' level of involvement before entering the war? How did the U.S. involvement influence the outcome of the war?
Problem solving	After reading about the Lewis and Clark expedition, what do you think was the biggest challenge that Meriwether Lewis and William Clark faced? How did they deal with this challenge? How would you have handled this situation in their place?	Could the Europeans and Native Americans have lived in peace? If yes, what compromises and agreements could have been put into place to avoid the slaughter and mass relocation of the Native Americans? If no, why not? Explain your answer with specific examples.	Consider the negative impacts of the Industrial Revolution, then focus on one negative byproduct— political, social, environmental, or economic—of the Industrial Revolution and think of ways this could have been mitigated.

Question Type	Upper Elementary School	Middle School	High School
Brainstorming	The Shang Dynasty is known as a period of great innovation. Brainstorm a list of new inventions, designs, and creations that appeared during the Shang Dynasty.	What reasons did the Europeans have for exploring and colonizing America? Brainstorm as many reasons as you can think of.	Brainstorm the ways that the United States Constitution has influenced contemporary political systems. Which countries have been influenced by the U.S. Constitution? How has the ideology in the U.S. Constitution been a model for other countries?
Debate	Of the following Greek scholars, who do you think had the biggest impact on Greek society and politics? What did this person study? What were his main ideas or teachings? What was his impact? • Socrates • Plato • Aristotle	Do you think Christopher Columbus is a historical figure we should celebrate with a national holiday? Why or why not?	The two dominant political parties in the United States are locked in a bitter debate over how to solve the country's budget deficit. Republicans advocate cutting spending and oppose tax increases. Democrats favor cost reductions but argue that new taxes are necessary to preserve important social programs. Which side do you favor and why? What points would you cite to support your view in a debate?

Science Question Grid

Question Type	Upper Elementary School	Middle School	High School
Subjective	How are both living and nonliving components of an ecosystem important to its delicate balance? Identify *one* ecosystem to focus on, then discuss the role of both the living and nonliving components. How do they complement one another? What happens if there is a lack of balance between these two components in an ecosystem?	Define the word "theory" in your own words. Use examples to make your explanation clear. Why is this term commonly misunderstood?	Most scientists agree that global warming is a fact and that it is largely caused by human activity such as burning fossil fuels. A smaller group of scientists argue that climate changes run in cycles and that the current warming trend is a natural cycle. What do you believe is causing the increasing temperatures on our planet?
Evaluative	What impact does the ocean have on the weather? How does the water cycle affect weather patterns?	What impact do genetic variation and environmental factors have on evolution? Do you think a species' genetic variation or environment has a larger impact on its evolution?	What role does the nervous system play in the body? How important is the nervous system to your overall health?
Problem solving	The global fresh water supply is limited. What can you do to make sure the fresh water reserves stay healthy? List specific things you can do in your daily life to conserve water.	Select an organism that has become extinct in the last 100 years. Identify the factors that led to that organism's extinction, then propose a plan that you think could have saved	Think about the negative impact humans have on their ecosystems. Select a specific ecosystem inhabited by humans, identify a negative impact of the human presence in that ecosystem, and propose real

Question Type	Upper Elementary School	Middle School	High School
	Think outside the box, and consider all the ways water is used.	that organism from extinction.	solutions you think would mitigate the negative impacts.
Brainstorming	Brainstorm metals, and label them as pure elements or as composed of a combination of elements. List all of the metals you can think of without looking at the periodic table. Use what you know about each to label them pure or combination.	Brainstorm a list of chemical reactions that you can observe in an average week. For each, briefly describe the chemical reactions taking place. What is the result of this reaction?	Describe the body's two "lines of defense" against disease. Consider internal and external defense mechanisms. Brainstorm three specific examples of how each line of defense would combat a possible infection.
Debate	Based on what you know about the characteristics of an herbivore versus a carnivore, do you think human beings are designed to be herbivores or carnivores?	Given what you know about genetics, do you think that scientists could or should clone cells and/or animals? Explain your position.	Do you believe the United States should be a leader in the quest to reduce global carbon emissions? Why or why not?

Math Question Grid

Question Type	Upper Elementary School	Middle School	High School
Subjective	How would understanding the concepts of mean, median, and mode help you interpret data sets? Use an example of a data set you would encounter in life,	Imagine you are shopping at the grocery store for your mom. She has asked you to get canned tomato sauce. One can is 24 ounces and costs x, but two 12-ounce cans cost y. How do you decide which is	Explain the difference between a rational number and an irrational number in your own words. When do you encounter rational numbers

(Continued)

(Continued)

Question Type	Upper Elementary School	Middle School	High School
	and explain how you would use mean, median, and mode to better understand the data.	the better deal? Explain the process by which you would come to an answer. Are there any other variables you might have to consider when making your decision?	in your life? When do you encounter irrational numbers? How are they similar to and different from one another?
Evaluative	You are at a grocery store, and the regular line has 1 person with 23 items, while the express line has 3 people with 4 items or less each. Which line will move faster? What variables might impact the pace of each line? Given these possible variables, which line would you choose to get into?	You get to decorate and decide on the arrangement of the furniture in your new bedroom. How important will angle measurements, area, surface area, and volume be in this process? Which concept would be most important to your job of deciding the layout of your room? Which concept would be least important or helpful in this process?	During the summer you decide to take sailing classes in the San Francisco Bay. You realize that you can apply your understanding of vectors to sailing. Explain how understanding vectors could help you to be a better sailor.
Problem solving	You are at the mall shopping with friends, and you have $50. You want to buy a CD for $12.68, a book for $7.42, and a computer game for $28.15. How would you work this problem out in your head if you did not have a calculator or a pen and paper? Do you have enough money?	Ask each member of your family to stretch out his or her arms horizontally. Measure each "arm span" from fingertip to fingertip. Record this information. Then measure the height of everyone in your house. Once you have both sets of measurements, use a linear equation to demonstrate your results. What did you learn about the	You are traveling with your family, and you will be visiting two countries outside of the United States. You want to buy a souvenir in one of the countries you are visiting, but you have a limited budget of $50 (U.S.). Write an algebraic expression to show how much

Question Type	Upper Elementary School	Middle School	High School
	Do you have change left over? Remember: This is a mental math problem, so no calculators!	relationship between these two measurements? What assumptions can you make about the general population based on this information?	your $50 will be worth in each of the two currencies. Solve each algebraic expression, and then explain where you will get more for your money. Where will you buy your souvenir?
Brainstorming	Brainstorm all of the ways you encounter fractions in your life. Then reflect on these examples you have shared, and write a short explanation of how fractions help you in your daily life.	You encounter a wide variety of numbers expressed in units in your life. Brainstorm a variety of examples of numbers that are expressed in units. After you have brainstormed as many units of measurements as you can, reflect on the units of measurement that you use most in your daily life. Use a specific example from your life to support your answer.	Brainstorm different ways to express 1.12^x using the properties of exponents. Which expression would be most useful when calculating a monthly interest rate? Why?
Debate	"The number of texts being sent is on the rise, especially among teenagers age 13 to 17. According to Nielsen, the average teenager now sends 3,339 texts per month" (Nielson Study, 2010). If a teen sends 3,339 text	Before writing a response to this question, roll a die 50 times and record which side it lands on each time. Analyze your results for any interesting trends, and think about what might have impacted your results. Do you think there is an equal chance that the die will	Do you think using the game Angry Birds would be an effective way to teach math? Why or why not? What principles of math are present in this game? How could examples from the game

(Continued)

(Continued)

Question Type	Upper Elementary School	Middle School	High School
	messages every month, how many text messages total would a teen send in a 12-month time period? Do you think this number is surprising?	land on any one of its six sides? Why or why not? Did your experiment impact your answer?	be applied to mathematical concepts you are studying?

Question Types That Kill Conversations

Following are some of the question types that discourage discussion and should be avoided when a teacher is attempting to engage students in dynamic conversations online.

Factual Questions

Factual questions have just one "right" answer, which must be supported by evidence, so they do not invite further discussion once a student answers the question correctly.

Information-Retrieval Questions

Information-retrieval questions ask students to find a particular piece of information from a source (e.g., textbook, online resource). Like factual questions, these types of questions do not encourage students to engage in discussions; once the correct answer is presented, there is nothing left to discuss.

Tips for Designing Strong Questions

Begin With an Eye-Catching Title

An eye-catching title helps to capture student interest. Instead of titling a discussion topic "Chapter 3 Question," begin with a catchy title such as "Should We Clone Human Beings?" or "Bizarre Photo: What Happened Here?" This draws students in and intrigues them. Use alliteration in your titles to create a poetic quality, and incorporate interesting vocabulary to excite curiosity.

Embed Media

Embedded media engages students. Have fun with photos and videos! Students love all things visual. Include pictures and video clips to present information, explain concepts, inspire debate, and stimulate creative writing. Embed Word documents with directions, lecture notes, vocabulary, and assignment descriptions to support student work online as well.

Layer Your Questions

Layer your questions to increase participation and differentiate instruction. A tiered question consists of multiple questions that build on one another and vary in complexity, thus giving students freedom to answer questions they understand or feel confident responding to.

Begin with a general question that leads to specific questions that narrow the scope of the conversation and encourage students to examine the issue/topic more closely. The broad "hook" question draws students in, but the more specific follow-up questions gives them the freedom to focus on the aspect of the topic they find most interesting. If the questions are more specific, then the responses are likely to be more specific.

Another approach to layering your questions is to begin with a content-specific question, then follow it with more general reflective questions that encourage students to connect the topic to their own lives. This strategy is particularly helpful in differentiating instruction online to engage a variety of skill levels.

The plethora of online tools available to educators can help make the seemingly impossible task of individualizing instruction more manageable. Teachers can use online discussion tools to present questions that are tiered, encouraging stronger students to answer the more complex nuances of the questions asked, while allowing struggling students to answer the simpler, more reflective questions and learn from the responses of their peers.

Example of a layered question:

Read the article "Spilled Oil" from the June 28, 2010, issue of the *New Yorker*, then identify and evaluate the bias. What bias is present? Where does this bias come from? How does this bias impact the way the content is presented? Is it possible to avoid bias in writing? Do you have a bias that influences your thoughts on the oil spill?

Questions that are layered offer students a variety of angles from which to answer questions. Students who are advanced might focus on the larger implications of the bias in this article in relation to society and government, while other students might discuss whether they believe bias in writing can be avoided. The trick is to give students the freedom to choose how they respond to a question by layering more complex questions on top of more reflective questions.

Ask Controversial or Polarizing Questions

Ask controversial or polarizing questions to draw students into a conversation or debate. If you have established a safe space online, then presenting controversial questions will allow students to engage in constructive discussions about topics they are passionate about. As a facilitator, you will need to follow the conversations closely to ensure students maintain a respectful tone when expressing opposing viewpoints. In Chapter 5 we discuss how you can successfully create a virtual safe space to ensure that communication in your online space is respectful and supportive.

Encourage Students to Make Connections

Encourage connections between your topic of discussion and students' life experiences. If students are able to connect the discussion to their families, friends, classes, books, music, interests, hobbies, and points of reference, then the information being discussed will be more meaningful and they will retain the information longer. Incorporating these connections into the conversations will also personalize the discussion and lead to more meaningful student interactions.

Be Flexible

Be flexible during discussions. Sometimes the conversation will head in a direction you did not anticipate. These tangential conversations can be just as valuable as the initial topics presented. It is important to evaluate each individual discussion and ask follow-up questions that keep students on track but do not pigeonhole their responses. Do not get locked into your agenda as a facilitator; instead be open to the organic evolution of conversations.

Focus on Topics of Interest to All Grade Levels

Focus on topics of interest to all grade levels by asking questions that appeal to all students, regardless of age. Questions on sports, music, television, current technology products, and fads in clothing styles, for example, pique the interest of students from upper elementary through high school. Those are subjects they discuss by choice on a daily basis. Incorporating those topics into your online discussions can encourage participation and increase interest.

What Does a Good Online Question Look Like?

Title: Does reading cure racism?   ⟵————— **Start with a catchy title**

Description: Do you agree with Angelou's statement that the only way we as a society will be free of the "blight of ignorance" is if we read and learn about African Heritage? Do you agree that reading, knowledge, and education are essential to respecting differences and forming cross-racial friendships? If so, why do you agree? If not, what do you think is crucial to eliminating ignorance between racial groups?

Type: Yes/No   **Layer questions**

Attach: Embed the video, "Maya Angelou: My Greatest Achievement."

Design different types of questions

Incorporate multimedia

Attachments

Maya Angelou Discusses Her Son

Maya Angelou: My Greatest Achievement
by visionaryproject

Chapter Summary

Designing curriculum is one of the most important aspects of the teaching presence in both the traditional class and in the work done online. Discussion questions and topics must be dynamic and able to drive meaningful discussions. When designing discussion questions, teachers should begin with an interesting title, include clear expectations for participation, embed media whenever possible, and layer their questions to invite a variety of responses. This is an art form that requires the teacher to capture student interest, inspire meaningful contributions, differentiate instruction, and foster discussions that will invite a variety of perspectives.

Book Study Questions

1. In your current practice, what type of question do you most commonly ask—factual, information retrieval, subjective, evaluative, reflective, problem solving, brainstorming, or debate? Why do you gravitate to this particular question type? What are your objectives in asking this type of question? Does asking this type of question effectively engage your students?

2. How will the question grids provided in this chapter support you in designing strong questions? Will you be able to use any of these questions with your own students? Are these questions similar to or different from the kinds of questions you currently ask? Explain.

3. When designing questions, do you think it is important to use different question structures (e.g., debate, multiple choice, forum)? How might structuring your conversations help to drive interesting discussions and retain student interest? If you have a learning platform or learning management system that does not offer a variety of question types, how can you design questions to create variety in your conversations to maintain student interest?

4. Are there any tips you would add to the section "Tips for Designing Strong Questions"? What additional strategies will you use to design questions that effectively engage your students?

Reference

Scott, S. (2008). Perceptions of students' learning critical thinking through debate in a technology classroom: A case study. *Journal of Technology Studies, 34*(1), 39–44. Retrieved from http://scholar.lib.vt.edu/ejournals/JOTS/

"U.S. Teen Mobile Report: Calling Yesterday, Texting Today, Using Apps Tomorrow." Nielsen Wire. 14 Oct 2010. Retrieved from http://blog.nielsen.com/nielsenwire/online_mobile/u-s-teen-mobile-report-calling-yesterday-texting-today-using-apps-tomorrow/

5

Develop a Dynamic Learning Community Online

Once a teacher has defined his or her own role in the online community, it is important to support students in developing their social presence online. Students must feel confident in their ability to participate in the class dialogue as valued and unique members of the group. This can be achieved if a safe space is created, clear expectations are established, and opportunities for relationship building are provided at the start of the work done online.

Creating and Maintaining a Safe Space Online

Most teachers begin the year by establishing clear guidelines for behavior and creating a safe environment in their physical classrooms to ensure students feel safe, supported, and respected. This necessary work done in the first month of school is critical to lowering students' affective filters and laying a strong foundation on which to build throughout the year.

Just as it is essential to begin the school year by creating a safe space in the physical classroom, establishing an online community must be done with intention if it is to be successful and sustainable. As Garrison (2007) states in "Online Community of Inquiry Review: Social, Cognitive, and Teaching Presence Issues," a sense of community is "essential to support collaborative learning and discourse associated with higher levels of learning" (p. 61). Creating this sense of community is not a simple task for the facilitator, but it is "significantly associated with perceived learning" (p. 61). When students feel safe in a community, they are able to begin forming "personal and purposeful relationships" (p. 63), which are the foundation of developing one's social presence. When a social presence is established within an online community, students perceive themselves as individuals who are capable of engaging with their peers in an authentic and meaningful way. This makes prioritizing the development of personal relationships fundamental at the start of any work online.

Many teachers who are "digital immigrants"—"not born into the digital world but have, at some later point in our lives, become fascinated by and adopted many or most of the new technology" (Prensky, 2001, pp. 1–2)—feel uncertain about their abilities to teach students how to engage online. It can be intimidating to teach using technology when a growing number of students are proficient users.

Mark Prensky (2001) first introduced the terms *digital natives* and *digital immigrants* to define today's students and, by contrast, their teachers. He argues that "our students today are all 'native speakers' of the digital language of computers, video games and the Internet" (p. 1). Despite being technology natives who regularly engage in this medium, students do not necessarily have the skills needed to communicate and collaborate with peers online. They spend hours updating Facebook pages, sending text messages, and e-mailing, but few students know how powerful their words are. They rapid-fire messages to "friends" but rarely see the look on the faces of people receiving those messages. It is critical to developing a social presence and respectful dialogue that they learn concrete strategies to support them in communicating in a supportive and substantive way. The best way to start is creating a clear set of guidelines for their interactions online.

The Dos and Don'ts of Student Communication Online

Establishing clear expectations for online interactions is a critical step in creating an online forum that will be successful in the long term. A stronger in-class community will form as a result of establishing and maintaining a safe space online.

Resource 5.1 presents the list of dos and don'ts I created for my classes to make my expectations for online communication clear. To be effective, your learning platform or learning management system (LMS) must be a safe space where students feel their voices will be respected, supported, and heard.

Resource 5.1   Dos and Don'ts of Student Communication Online

Name_____ Date_____

Dos and Don'ts of Student Communication Online

Strategies for creating and maintaining a safe space:

- **Use each other's names.** Using a person's name when you respond to his or her postings creates a friendly tone online.
- **Read questions and conversational postings carefully** to avoid unnecessary confusion.
- **Compliment your peers** when they post strong responses or contribute original ideas.
- **Ask questions.** If anything is unclear or you want further information or insight on a topic, just ask. If *you* have a question, there are probably other members of the group who are confused and need further clarification as well. Remember, there is no such thing as a dumb question.
- **Be considerate.** Remember that your peers cannot see your body language or hear your tone of voice, so you need to keep your language direct and respectful.
- **Avoid slang and jargon.** Some slang or jargon may be familiar to you, but not to others.
- **No sarcasm.** Sarcasm is negative and can lead to tensions and hurt feelings online. Keep language clear and concise.
- **Listen to all ideas presented.** Remember, there are no right or wrong answers in a discussion, and a variety of perspectives adds depth.
- **Stay open-minded.** If you expect others to respect and consider your comments and ideas, you must do the same for them.

- **Respond instead of reacting.** Do not write a response if you are angry or upset. Instead, wait until you have had time to calm down and collect your thoughts before responding.
- *Really* **read your peers' responses.** Avoid skimming. Respect the time your peers have spent articulating their thoughts by reading carefully and thoughtfully.
- **Reread your messages before sending** them to ensure that your ideas are clearly communicated and supported.
- **Critique the content**, not the person. Focus on what has been said, not the person who said it.
- **Do not present your personal opinions as fact.** Back up your ideas with information (i.e., details, evidence, and examples) to strengthen your statements.
- **Courteously answer all questions** addressed directly to you.
- **Make "I" statements when respectfully disagreeing.** Sharing an opposing opinion or idea is an important part of discussion, but it needs to be presented in a constructive manner that encourages further discussion.
- **Do not use all caps** when writing; it is interpreted as yelling.
- **Avoid emotional punctuation**, like exclamation points, unless you are complimenting an idea shared.

Source: Democrasoft, http://www.democrasoft.com

I suggest reviewing this list in class and allowing students to practice example scenarios in small groups. Then post this list as a resource for reference in your online forum. In addition to clearly outlining what you want your students to do and not do online, modeling the actual language supports students in a smooth transition online.

Providing a variety of sentence starters that show students how to build on another student's point, respectfully disagree with an idea, or compliment a peer is helpful prior to work done online. It provides the language "training wheels" that support students in articulating their thoughts in the beginning of their work online. Once they are proficient in respectful online dialogue, they will use these starters automatically and adapt them. Students can practice these skills more effectively if they can refer to a list like the one in Resource 5.2.

Resource 5.2   Strong Sentence Starters

Name_____ Date_____

Strong Sentence Starters

Use the following examples as a guide for your own replies to peers online. Remember to use each other's names and maintain a respectful tone in your conversations.

Rebecca's comment made me think about . . .

Although Rio made a strong point that _____, I think . . .

I respectfully disagree with Zach's assertion that _____, because . . .

I really appreciate Cyrus' insight into . . .

Thank you, Manuel, for sharing . . .

I had not thought about Leigh's point that . . .

Great point, Zahara! Have you considered . . . ?

Even though Dalia's point is valid, I tend to . . .

Building on Lawrence's statement that . . .

In contrast to Michelle's point . . .

Bradley highlighted some key ideas when he said . . .

Lulu, can you clarify your statement that _____?

Carmen, your posting reminded me of . . .

Nadya's observation that _____ reflects . . .

Given what you know about _____, Darius, what are your thoughts on _____?

Marcella, do you agree (or disagree) with . . . ?

Robin, how would you define . . . ?

Like Amaya, I also connected _____ to _____.

Source: Democrasoft, http://www.democrasoft.com

I post my "Dos and Don'ts of Student Online Communication" and "Strong Sentence Starters" on our Collaborize Classroom site for students to reference throughout the year. I suggest that teachers post their expectations to their learning platform so students and parents have access to them at all times.

Creating a Class Code of Conduct

Creating a code of conduct that clearly establishes a list of behaviors for online engagement and communication also makes expectations visible and creates shared agreements within the community. Including students in the process of generating the content for your code of conduct creates buy-in as well. If students feel they had a voice in the process, then they will be more invested in maintaining the safe space in their online discussions.

Resource 5.3 is a template for teachers to adapt in creating their own student code of conduct. If you want students to actively participate in this process, use class time to organize them into small groups to brainstorm behaviors they think will create and maintain a safe space online. Some teachers prefer to identify behaviors they consider nonnegotiable, then allow students to complete the list.

When I designed my own code of conduct agreement, I spent time in class brainstorming expectations. I then used the multi-multiple-choice option on my Collaborize Classroom site to post all of their suggestions. Then students were able to select their top five favorite suggestions, and I published the results to the Results Page, which created a colorful chart clearly identifying their top choices as a class. I included their top five choices in my class code of conduct.

Then I had each student sign the Student Code of Conduct Agreement. Because they participated in developing the code, they had a vested interest in it. As a result they were more willing to agree to and follow the dictates of the code—more so than if I had generated it and presented it to them as a done deal.

Resource 5.3   Example Online Student Code of Conduct Agreement

Ms. Tucker's Student Code of Conduct

You will regularly engage in discussions and collaborative group work with your peers. To maintain a safe space online, we need to agree to uphold specific behaviors to ensure our online space stays respectful and supportive.

I,_____,agree to:

[Neatly print your first and last name]

- Actively engage in the conversations taking place online.
- Read and think deeply about my peers' ideas, questions, suggestions, and comments.
- Address my classmates by name when responding to their ideas.
- Maintain an appropriate tone and stay on topic.
- Respectfully disagree with ideas. I will not criticize my peers because their ideas are different from or contrary to my own.
- Be open-minded. I believe I can learn from the diversity of perspectives in this class.
- Attempt to think "outside of the box" to present new ideas and perspectives.
- Respect the privacy of my peers. I will not republish (i.e., cut and paste content from our discussions to other social networking forums) or discuss conversations that take place in our class portal.
- Support my classmates in their learning process. I will not tease or make fun of my peers or their ideas.
- Encourage discussion by asking interesting, thought-provoking questions.
- Seek help from my peers and/or teacher if I have concerns or questions.
- Only attach information and media that is appropriate to the educational setting.
- Submit work that is reflective of my intellect. I will follow the appropriate conventions of English (i.e., spelling, grammar, sentence structure, word choice, etc.) to ensure that my postings clearly communicate my ideas.

My signature verifies that I have read, understand, and agree to comply with the above code of conduct. I understand that I must play an active role in establishing and maintaining a safe online space to ensure that all students feel comfortable actively participating.

If I violate any of the above expectations for my conduct in our online portal, I am aware that I will be held accountable for jeopardizing our safe space online.

Student Signature _____

Parent Signature _____

_____

Source: Democrasoft, http://www.democrasoft.com

If a student violates the safe space established, it is important to address that violation immediately. In my class, the first violation leads to a conversation between my student and me to discuss what was said and why it was not appropriate given our code of conduct. After that discussion, I ask the student to complete a written reflection on what he or she said, why it jeopardized our safe space, and how he or she can avoid doing this in the future (see Resource 5.4). If the behavior continues, I repeat the first step, then communicate with the parent about his or her child's behavior.

Resource 5.4   Example Safe Space Reflection Form

Name_____ Date_____

Safe Space Violation Reflection

This is a required assignment. Please complete this reflection to the best of your ability. Please think about and thoughtfully answer the following questions:

- How did your behavior jeopardize the safe space expectations established for our online discussions?
- How might your behavior have made your classmates feel?
- Do you believe that your behavior was an accurate reflection of who you are as a person?
- How can you ensure that this type of violation does not happen again in our online discussions?

_____

_____

_____

_____

_____

_____

_____

_____

_____

_____

_____

_____

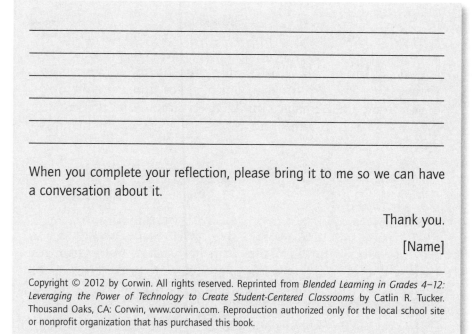

When you complete your reflection, please bring it to me so we can have a conversation about it.

Thank you.

[Name]

Each teacher must develop a system of consequences that works for him or her. I have only had to use my safe space reflection form once in two years, when a student made a sarcastic comment that did not translate online and led to hurt feelings. In addition to speaking with the student and asking her to complete a reflection, I used it as a teachable moment in class to discuss why slang and sarcasm should be avoided online. The conversation was extremely positive and culminated in the student in question apologizing. It was heartfelt and genuine. She had not considered how her words might impact the other student she was addressing. Given how much of their discourse takes place via electronic mediums, it is critical that students have opportunities to practice these communication skills with guidance and support from teachers.

Visually Display Your Expectations for Participation on Your Site

In addition to the guidelines you set for behavior, it is important to define participation requirements. Students need to have a place online to reference your participation expectations for a given unit. For example, I use a "Welcome" banner on my Collaborize Classroom site to clearly outline the number of postings and replies required each night during a given unit.

Example

> Welcome to our Collaborize Classroom site! You are required to post *two* substantive postings each night in response to discussion questions and post a minimum of *two* comments to your peers. Your postings should reflect time, energy, and effort. Remember, this is a digital extension of our classroom. Please be open-minded and respectful in your interactions with your peers.
>
> Thank you.
>
> Ms. Tucker

This visual reminder answers the ever-present question: "What are we supposed to do?" Despite your best efforts to be clear, some students will forget what they have been asked to do and/or what the expectations are. Let your site do the work for you in addressing these questions.

Once you have covered your expectations for student communication online, agreed on a class code of conduct, and set up a visual reminder on your site, you are ready to facilitate online icebreakers so students can practice these new skills, form relationships, and develop their social presence online.

Building an Online Community

Every teacher has experienced the sinking feeling that accompanies a moment in the second half of the school year when a student does not know the name of another student in the class, despite sharing a room for months. Teachers internalize this as their failure to create opportunities for students to get to know one another at the start of the school year. Most teachers value icebreakers and love the idea of encouraging relationships between students. Unfortunately, the time it takes to facilitate these fun activities is usually sacrificed due to time constraints. Teachers feel immense pressure to get started on their curriculum at the beginning of the year to ensure they get through it all.

Another reason some teachers, including me, hesitate to start the year off with a variety of unstructured fun activities is that they are attempting to establish a *tone* for the class in the first few weeks of school. Icebreakers invite informal, loud, chaotic conversations that can be challenging to manage when a teacher is just getting to know students and establishing acceptable behaviors in class.

Break the Ice Online

Online discussions can free teachers from the time constraints and classroom management concerns that tend to curb these social "get to know each other" activities. They also provide a space for students to engage in these conversations without creating chaos in the physical classroom.

Plus, these nonacademic conversations are a great opportunity to practice the "Dos and Don'ts of Student Online Communication." Teachers can pull examples of strong responses and share them with students as examples of what they should strive toward. Missteps online can also be gently highlighted and corrected to ensure they do not continue.

Five Student Icebreakers Adapted for an Online Community

Here are five student icebreakers that are compatible with an online discussion forum. My Collaborize Classroom site allows me to create different question types, so teachers using other sites will need to tailor these icebreakers to fit their individual learning platform.

1. Time Machine

If you could travel in time to one of the following periods in American history, which would you choose and why? After selecting the time period you would visit, explain your choice in two to four sentences.

- 1960s Hippie Generation/Anti-War Movement/Civil Rights Movement
- 1830s Wild West Era
- 2025 Future
- 1980s Wild Fashion/Brat Pack/Punk Rock
- 1950s Rock n' Roll/Suburbia
- 1920s Roaring 20s
- 1970s Disco Fever

Once you have posted your response, reply thoughtfully to *at least three* of your peers.

2. Two Truths and a Lie

Write three statements about yourself. Two of your statements should be true, and one should be made up. In your response list three statements, so your peers can guess which statement is the "lie" in their reply to you. Be creative!

Once you have posted your three statements for the group, read the statements posted by your peers and reply thoughtfully to *at least three* of your peers. In each reply, identify the statement you believe is false and explain your choice.

3. Super Power

If you could have any super power, which would you choose and why?

- Read minds
- Stop time
- Fly
- Become invisible
- Heal people

Once you have posted your response, reply thoughtfully to *at least three* of your peers.

4. Famous Person

If you could meet one famous person (dead or alive), who would you choose and why? State the person's name and occupation (i.e., politician, comedian, musician, author, etc.), explain why you want to meet this person, and list *three* questions you would like to ask him or her.

Once you have posted your response, reply thoughtfully to *at least three* of your peers. If one of your peers wants to meet someone you also admire, feel free to post suggestions for questions he or she might ask this person.

5. Desert Island Dilemma

If you knew you would be stranded on a desert island for one year, which *three* objects would you bring with you? Keep in mind that there is *no* electricity on the island! Choose your objects carefully, then explain your choices in a short paragraph.

Once you have completed your selections and posted your explanation, read and respond to *at least three* peers.

Beginning with fun, informal questions hooks those reluctant students who may not be enthusiastic or do homework consistently. If conversations take place in class about fun discussions that happened online, it may pique the interest of those students on the sidelines who have not yet participated online. Online icebreakers encourage students to connect on a personal level while using each other's names, developing thoughtful replies, and practicing questioning skills. My students enjoyed icebreakers so much that they are still requesting them well into second semester.

Five Parent-Student Icebreakers Adapted for an Online Community

If you are working with younger students, it is a good idea to start with student-parent icebreakers. This inspires a dialogue between the students and their parents. It also helps introduce the parents to the online space so they feel comfortable about the work being done online.

1. What Was Your Mom or Dad's Favorite Subject Growing Up?

Talk to one or both of your parents. Find out what subject they enjoyed most in school and why. Select the subject they chose, then post a response describing their answer. Compare their choice to your favorite subject now.

- English
- History
- Science
- Math
- Health
- Foreign Language

After you have posted your answer, read your classmates' postings and reply thoughtfully to *at least two* people.

2. Who Influenced Your Parents the Most?

Ask your parent about the *one* person who influenced him or her most growing up. In your response identify the person who impacted your parent, and explain why this person affected you mom or dad so greatly. Then reflect on this. Did you know this person?

After you have posted your answer, read your classmates' postings and reply thoughtfully to *at least two* people.

3. One Piece of Life Advice

Ask your parents what *one* piece of advice they would give you about life based on their own experiences.

Post their piece of advice for the class. Then read the advice of other parents, and vote for your favorite. Post a reply to the student who posted the life advice you found most helpful or interesting. Explain why you liked the advice.

4. Family Fun—Is This a Vacation You Want to Go On?

Ask your parents where they would want to go if they could plan a family trip without worrying about money.

- Where would you go? Why?
- How long would you stay?
- What would you see?
- How would you travel—plane, train, boat, car, RV?
- Who would you invite?

After you have posted your answer, read your classmates' postings and reply thoughtfully to *at least two* people.

5. Parent Playlist

Ask your parents what three songs (title and artist) they would include on a soundtrack of their lives. Explain why they chose each song.

- What does it remind them of?
- What deeper significance does it have for them?

After you have posted your answer, read your classmates' postings and reply thoughtfully to *at least two* people.

Note: There are additional online icebreakers at www.corwin.com/blendedlearning4-12.

Start Simply to Cement Routines and Correct First Missteps

As with any new routine or skill set, there are bound to be small set-backs. I am always asked how I handle missteps online. Quite simply, I embrace those moments as opportunities to revisit expectations for online behavior, interactions, and communication.

In the first few weeks of school, when our online work and discussions are new to students, I regularly highlight examples of strong work online and work that needs development. I do this using student samples (no names). Since I have no technology in my actual classroom, I copy and paste examples from our online discussions into a Word document, then make a transparency to show students. Teachers with the luxury of projectors can easily project the examples onto a screen or white board to make this process simpler.

It can be even more effective to allow students to discover what strong participation looks like or identify missteps online for them-selves. I have done this by creating a handout with a selection of online postings, then I put students in groups and ask them to iden-tify what was done well in each posting and what could be improved. This requires students to evaluate and think critically about what they are reading. Students never fail to impress me with their astute observations of the strong elements present in writing as well as their detailed suggestions for improvement.

Using in-class time to facilitate this work also communicates to students that the work done online is not separate from the work completed in class. It reinforces the reality that online work is a digital extension of the work done in class.

As an English teacher, I also stress the importance of maintain-ing the conventions of English while working online. I do not want my students using text message language or failing to use para-graph breaks just because work is done online. Even though they communicate digitally all the time, many students lapse into a quasi-English that does not resemble the writing I hope to see in my English class.

I created the document "Avoid Mechanical Missteps in Online Communication" to combat some of this quasi-English (Resource 5.5). It is the individual teacher's choice to establish the expectations and norms that best fit his or her class. For some, the formal nature of this document may not be necessary.

Resource 5.5   Avoid Mechanical Missteps in Online Communication

Name_____ Date_____

Avoid Mechanical Missteps in Online Communication

Remember that our online discussion platform is an extension of our physical classroom. Your writing should reflect time, energy, and editing. Please review the following.

Capitalization

- Always capitalize "I" when speaking in first person.
- Capitalize the first letter of sentences, the first letter of your peers' names, titles (*To Kill a Mockingbird*), and all proper nouns (i.e., specific names of people, places, and events).

Punctuation Problems

- Remember to use a question mark when you ask a question.
- Do not overuse exclamation marks. They should be used sparingly for emphasis.
- Apostrophes are needed to indicate possession (e.g., Christine's comment made me consider an alternative perspective.).
- When quoting, periods and commas go inside quotation marks.

Commonly Confused Words

- *Then vs. Than.* "Then" indicates a sequence of time, and "than" is used for comparison (e.g., We went to the museum and then had lunch. I like action movies better than romance movies.).
- *Accept vs. Except.* "Accept" is a verb that means "to receive, admit, regard as true, or say yes." "Except" is a preposition that means "to exclude" (e.g., I accept the truth in your statement. I ate everything except my peas.).
- *Loose vs. Lose.* "Loose" is an adjective, the opposite of "tight." "Lose" is a verb meaning to no longer have possession of or to misplace (e.g., If your pants are too loose, you might lose your pants.).

- *Lay vs. Lie.* Use "lay" when there is a direct object, and use "lie" when there is no direct object (e.g., I lay my books on the table. I lie down when I am tired.).
- *Raise vs. Rise.* Use "raise" when there is a direct object, and use "rise" when there is no direct object (e.g., I raise my hand in class. The sun will rise each morning.).
- *Who vs. Whom.* "Who" is a pronoun used in the place of a subject, and "whom" is a pronoun used in place of an object (e.g., Who is coming for dinner? Whom did you invite for dinner?).

Homophone Errors

- *Who's vs. Whose.* "Who's" is the contraction for "who is," and "whose" is the possessive of "who" (e.g., Who's coming to the party? Whose purse is this?).
- *Weather vs. Whether.* "Weather" is a noun referring to the atmospheric conditions in a specific place, and "whether" is a conjunction that introduces possibilities or alternatives (e.g., The weather outside will determine whether we go swimming or not.).
- *Your vs. You're.* "Your" is a possessive pronoun (e.g., your house), and "you're" is the contraction meaning "you are."
- *There vs. They're vs. Their.* "There" is used as a pronoun or to refer to a place, "they're" is the contraction for "they are," while "their" is a possessive pronoun (e.g., I put it over there. They're coming to the party. I read their blog.).
- *It's vs. Its.* "Its" is a possessive pronoun, and "it's" is the contraction for "it is" (e.g., It's a beautiful day for a walk. The dog pulled its leash.).
- *To vs. Too.* "To" is a preposition. "Too" means "also" or "to an excessive extent or degree" (e.g., I want help, too. It is too hot to eat.).

Spelling Errors

- Always spellcheck your work prior to posting. Spelling errors distract your reader from the quality of your content.
- "A lot" is always two words.

Using Italics vs. Quotes

- When referring to a book title, large publication (such as a book, magazine, or newspaper), or movie title, *italicize* it.
- When referring to a poem, short story, or article, use quotation marks.

Sentence Structure

- Keep sentences clear and concise.
- Avoid sentence fragments that fail to communicate a complete thought.
- Break up long sentences to avoid unnecessarily lengthy and confusing sentences.

Each subject has norms for communication, so I encourage teachers to articulate those subject-specific norms for students in the "Avoid Mechanical Missteps in Online Communication" document.

Teach Students to Say Something Substantial

One of the biggest challenges teachers face across disciplines is getting students to develop their explanations, ideas, and reasoning. In English I am constantly trying to motivate students to develop their writing and analysis. Too often the writing I receive is shallow and underdeveloped. When I introduced online discussions and group work, I faced similar challenges getting my students to respond to questions and to each other in substantive and meaningful ways.

I began by emphasizing that each posting should effectively drive conversation and motivate the other members of the group to think more deeply about the topic being discussed. To effectively support students in accomplishing this goal, it is essential that teachers make their expectations for student responses clear before initiating online conversations or activities.

If students understand *why* they are being asked to do something, they are more likely to do it. Explain that your learning platform or LMS is a place for them to engage in conversations, activities, and collaboration. If they actively participate in the online forum, it will support and strengthen their understanding of the curriculum.

Students must feel that the online forum is their space; as such, it is crucial that each member of the class/group take an active role in ensuring a high quality of discussion. Providing concrete strategies gives students confidence in their ability to participate in a meaningful and substantive way. Review the strategies in Resource 5.6 with your students in the early stages of their work online.

Resource 5.6   Say Something Substantial

Name_____ Date_____

Say Something Substantial

This is a list of strategies you can use when responding to questions and/or replying to your peers online to ensure that your contributions will drive discussions forward.

A substantial posting will do the following:

- Present a new question for discussion to broaden, refine, or redirect the conversation.
- Discuss a personal experience (i.e., memory, interaction, class, book, etc.) that has influenced your perception of a given topic. Provide specific details about where your ideas, beliefs, and/or opinions come from to support your statements.
- Think outside the box or play devil's advocate (respectfully, of course). Providing another point of view on a topic can spark further discussion.
- Ask your peers for clarification if ideas are presented that you do not clearly understand. Your peers are valuable resources.
- Make connections between the discussions taking place and information learned in other classes and subject areas. Connecting what you are learning to past knowledge or experiences will strengthen your retention of that information.
- Share a resource that has been helpful to you. Use the attachment feature to share images, documents, and videos that will add to the conversation.
- Summarize the main ideas being discussed in your own words to ensure you have a strong grasp of the central concepts. This will support your peers' learning as well.
- Comment thoughtfully and respectfully on the ideas, experiences, and questions presented by your peers. The more you engage with your peers, the more meaningful the conversations will be for everyone involved.

Source: Democrasoft, http://www.democrasoft.com

Defining what constitutes a substantial posting and then providing concrete strategies to support students in composing substantive responses will benefit the students' writing and discourse across disciplines.

Once you have provided strategies for students to use in responding substantively and modeled what a strong response looks like, the next step is teaching students how to end their postings in a way that invites further conversation. I provide "Eight Intriguing Exit Strategies that Continue the Conversation" (Resource 5.7) to guide students in this process.

Resource 5.7   Eight Intriguing Exit Strategies That Continue the Conversation

Name_____ Date_____

Eight Intriguing Exit Strategies That Continue the Conversation

Use the strategies below to practice ending your postings to invite peer responses. Each strategy is followed by an example. These exit strategies can be used in your original responses to the questions or in your replies to your peers. The goal is to make it easier for your classmates to build on the ideas you have presented.

- Propose a new idea for feedback.

  "Did anyone else reach a different conclusion based on the reading?"

- Ask for clarification or further explanation about an aspect of the question you had trouble answering.

  "I am confused about _____. Does anyone have any ideas or insights that might help me understand?"

- Ask your peers to make a connection between the topic and another piece of literature, a movie, or something they have personally experienced.

  "I was able to relate this to _____. Did anyone else make an interesting connection to the topic?"

- Invite your peers to draw a different conclusion or share another perspective.

  "Did anyone else reach a different conclusion or have a different perspective on this topic?"

- If you presented an opinion or idea about the given topic that was not addressed in the question, ask your peers to respond to it.

  "This topic was not presented in the question, but does anyone have an opinion about _____?"

- Pose a follow-up question to the group to expand the conversation or shift it in a new direction.

  "Answering this question made me wonder _____?"

- Present a controversial idea or statement, and ask your peers if they agree or disagree with the statement.

  "It seems like most of the class believes _____. Has anyone considered _____?"

- Encourage your peers to ask questions about the points you made if anything was confusing or unclear.

  "I had a hard time articulating my ideas. Does anyone have a question about my posting or the ideas I communicated in my posting?"

Source: Democrasoft, http://www.democrasoft.com

Just as I suggested you provide students with sentence starters to begin their conversations, I also think it is important to provide students with example sentences to teach them how to end a posting in a way that it invites responses. Ending a posting or reply in this way lets students know that it is okay to question or even contradict what was said by offering a different perspective. With time these become automatic habits, but students need a place to begin. They appreciate the opening to respond when participating in discussions, which reinforces their willingness to also end their own postings with these strategies that drive deeper, richer, more meaningful exchanges.

This critical work done at the beginning of the year helps your students establish their social presence online and creates a foundation of mutual respect and support that will result in the long-term success of your blended instruction model. This strong foundation created when you establish clear expectations, model language, and provide clear strategies for success will enable you to eventually expand your work online to include collaborative group work and student-driven projects.

Chapter Summary

To create a community of inquiry that successfully engages students in meaningful discourse, a teacher must first support students in developing their social presence. Social presence is the students' awareness both of themselves as unique contributors to a dialogue and of their peers. Beginning work online by clearly establishing expectations for behavior is an important first step to guiding students in this process. Provide a list of dos and don'ts for behavior and sentence starters that demonstrate respectful, supportive, and substantive communication online. Identify your shared agreements in a class code of conduct agreement to ensure a safe space online will be maintained by all members of the community. Once expectations for behavior and participation online have been clearly stated, reviewed, and discussed, actively build an online community using icebreakers to form relationships and practice this new skill set. Provide strategies for responding substantively in discussions, then use examples from the work online to model strong responses.

Following these steps at the beginning of work online will provide the necessary foundation for students to ensure they are successful in developing the social presence needed to create a community of inquiry.

Book Study Questions

1. How can developing a social presence online help students be successful in their interactions with their peers? In what ways can developing a social presence improve a student's self-esteem and self-confidence? How might developing a social presence in a community with students you know combat cyberbullying?

2. What strategies do you use to create a safe space in your physical classroom? Can you adapt any of these practices for the online space? If so, which ones? If not, why not?

3. How can you ensure students maintain a safe space online? Will you develop a clear set of consequences for misbehavior online? What types of consequences will you use to deal with safe space violations? How will you make this visible for students? When will you address missteps as a group, and when will you address them individually?

4. Will you engage your students in the process of identifying the behaviors you want to list in your "Dos and Don'ts of Student Communication Online" and "Class Code of Conduct"? Why or why not? What are the benefits of involving students in this process? What might be challenging about allowing students a voice in this process?

5. How will you make your expectations for daily/weekly participation visible on your site? How often do you plan to engage your students online? How might consistent expectations be helpful for students? Would regular engagement online add to or diminish the students' perceived value of work done? Explain.

6. How do you support relationship building in your physical classroom? Do you use icebreakers that you can adapt for the online space? If so, which icebreakers do you use that might work in an online environment?

7. How can you use the work done during online icebreakers to correct missteps and model strong responses in class? Brainstorm in-class activities that will effectively correct common missteps and help students improve the quality of their responses.

8. How might building a strong online community positively impact your students' interactions in class? What behaviors would you expect to transfer from the work online into your classroom? How can you support the transfer of positive behaviors from the online space into the classroom and vice versa?

9. How will teaching students strategies for contributing substantively positively impact the quality of their online dialogue? How will it positively impact their overall academic

performance? What challenges do you anticipate in teaching students how to engage substantively?

10. Are there subject-specific norms you plan to enforce in your online discussions and interactions? If so, what are they and how will you make them visible to students?

References

Garrison, D. R. (2007). Online community of inquiry review: Social, cognitive, and teaching presence issues. *Journal of Asynchronous Learning Networks, 11*(1), 61–72.

Prensky, M. (2001). Digital natives, digital immigrants. *On the Horizon, 9*(5), 1–6.

Sallnäs, E. L., Rassmus-Gröhn, K., & Sjöström, C. (2000). Supporting presence in collaborative environments by haptic force feedback. *ACM Transactions on Computer-Human Interaction, 7*(4), 461–476.

Introduction to Chapters 6 Through 9

Chapters 6 through 9 provide educators teaching English, history/social studies, science, and math in Grades 4 through 12 with clear examples of how an online learning platform or learning management system can be used to engage students in dynamic discussions, writing assignments, research, and collaborative group work. The benefit of using blended instruction with students continuously from elementary through high school is that teachers can gradually increase the rigor of online work to ensure students are able to demonstrate competency by the end of each year.

The questions designed for Chapters 6 through 9 are anchored in the new Common Core State Standards, which "establish clear and consistent goals for learning that will prepare America's children for success in college and work" (Common Core State Standards Initiative, 2011, para. 1). This shift to a national set of standards creates opportunities for states to align their teaching to ensure all students, regardless of location or socioeconomic status, are learning critical skills needed for success after secondary school. The Standards spell out what students should know and be able to do; they do not define how teachers are supposed to teach. These chapters provide strategies for how a blended learning model can be used to successfully teach the skills identified in the Common Core State Standards in each of the four primary subjects: English, history/social studies, science, and math.

Each subject-specific chapter is broken into three sections based on grade level: upper elementary school, middle school, and high school. I have designed two online activities for each grade level, so educators can see what assignments look like in an online environment. I have included high-resolution screenshots from my own Collaborize Classroom site. Teachers can recreate these types of discussions and writing activities using a variety of learning platforms and learning management systems.

Most teachers are quite comfortable introducing concepts in the classroom, but teachers new to a blended learning model need support taking work online to engage students in collaborative discussions and activities. Weaving online work back into the classroom with student-centered activities is the second aspect of the blended learning model that presents challenges for traditional teachers. I have structured Chapters 6 through 9 so that they focus on these two points of challenge: creating engaging online activities and weaving that online work back into the classroom.

I designed these chapters so that they present example online activities for teachers to use as a model for planning their own online assignments. Each online activity is followed by three in-class lesson ideas to demonstrate how the content introduced online can be effectively woven back into the classroom with student-centered activities. These activities are not intended to be complete lessons, but rather inspiration for teachers who want to build on the work done in the online environment. Online discussions and group work make it possible for teachers to use precious class time to facilitate learning opportunities in which students apply their understanding of concepts and work together on collaborative tasks—maximizing the potential of the group. These extension activities range from debates to writing assignments to group discussions to hands-on creative tasks. The objective of these student-centered in-class activities is to place students at the center of the learning process, encouraging higher levels of engagement with the curriculum and producing more meaningful learning outcomes.

Chapters 6 Through 9 Are Based on the Following Assumptions

1. Group work is best when groups are small to ensure all participants have an opportunity to be heard and play an active role in the group task. When I say small groups, I mean three to four students.

2. Students can be grouped by ability, interest, learning style, language proficiency, or at random—depending on the task. It is important to decide on grouping strategies in advance to best support students at all levels. Teachers should determine which method of grouping will result in the best learning outcomes.

3. Discussions are most effective when students have had an opportunity to think about a topic or issue, articulate a response, and hear what their peers have to say. Even class discussions work best when they start in small groups first, then extend to whole-class conversations.

4. Designing in-class activities that allow students to work together in groups to problem solve, research, and think critically prepares them for the communication and collaboration skills needed beyond high school. These are skills at the heart of the College and Career Readiness Standards, which are the backbone of the Common Core State Standards.

5. It is critical that teachers build a strong foundation of respect and trust prior to asking students to share personal and possibly sensitive information. Reflective questions that ask students to draw on their own life experiences will be unsuccessful if students do not feel safe in the online environment. These types of questions can build class community and bring students together, but to do so everyone must feel safe and supported.

6. Access to technology in classrooms varies. Many of the artistic assignments and projects described in the "Weave Online Work Into the Classroom With Student-Centered Activities" sections are designed for a classroom without technology. However, they can easily be taken online using creative tools for teachers with access to technology in their classrooms. I have included online resources, links, and tools for teachers who are able to use technology in the classroom.

Teaching the Common Core State Standards Using Blended Learning

The Common Core State Standards are woven throughout Chapters 6 through 9 to demonstrate how teachers can address these new

Standards within a blended learning model. Each grade-level section begins by clearly identifying the Standards addressed in the online examples in that section of the chapter. Along with each standard, I include the explanation of that standard taken directly from the Common Core State Standards Initiative website (www.core standards.org). Then I follow each online activity by listing the abbreviated version of each standard addressed by that specific task.

The Common Core State Standards require students as early as fourth grade to "use technology, including the Internet, to produce and publish writing as well as interact and collaborate with others" (Standard W.4.6). Using a learning platform in the upper elementary grades can help teachers support students in communicating and collaborating in a safe online environment to develop reading, writing, and language fluency skills, which are the Standards' goal.

The Standards also prioritize speaking and listening skills. They want students to "engage effectively in a range of collaborative discussions" (Standard SL.5.1), but as any teacher can attest, it is challenging to facilitate real-time conversations in class that include the majority of students. Beginning discussions online, where students have time to process the information, write a thoughtful response, and engage with their peers, gives them confidence, which makes it easier to jump into a rapidly moving in-class discussion. Online discussions, in general, make it possible for the teacher to start an in-class discussion at a deeper level because students have had a chance to engage online first.

Chapters 6 through 9 demonstrate how using the online space frees teachers up to design in-class learning opportunities that are more student centered. These chapters do not attempt to cover every standard for every grade level, but they do strive to provide teachers with examples of question structures that will serve to inspire their use of an online learning platform while addressing the Standards.

Reference

Common Core State Standards Initiative. (2011). *National Governors Association and State Education Chiefs launch common state academic standards.* Retrieved from http://www.corestandards.org/articles/8-national-governors -association-and-state-education-chiefs-launch-common-state-academic -standards

6

English Language Arts

The Common Core State Standards for English Language Arts are divided into two main categories: reading and writing. In upper elementary grades the reading standards focus on reading literature, informational texts, and foundational skills. The standards for reading literature and informational texts emphasize the importance of exposing students to a wide range of texts and tasks. The foundational skills foster students' "understanding and working knowledge of concepts of print, the alphabetic principle, and other basic conventions of the English writing system" (Reading Standards: Foundational Skills: Introduction). In middle school the foundational skills are dropped, indicating that by sixth grade students should have demonstrated proficiency in basic language skills. The reading literature and informational text standards continue through high school, becoming increasingly more challenging.

The reading standards must be taught in conjunction with the writing standards, which focus on three specific types of writing: opinion/argument, informative/explanatory, and narrative. Students must be able to convey ideas clearly, edit and revise their writing, conduct research, and use technology to produce and publish their work. Each year students need to "demonstrate increasing sophistication in all aspects of language use, from vocabulary and syntax to development and organization of ideas" (Writing Standards: Introduction), which requires that they write frequently.

In this chapter, I have designed online discussion questions and writing tasks that combine the reading and writing standards for each grade level to demonstrate how teachers can address multiple standards simultaneously using an online environment. The online activities require students to produce writing based on texts they have read. I have used texts specifically identified in the Common Core State Standards as those "illustrating the complexity, quality and range of student reading" (Standard 10). This writing then leads to a more in-depth discussion of the topic because students are encouraged to compliment, question, and build on each other's contributions. This conversation drives a deeper level of engagement and requires that students communicate clearly and coherently to be understood.

Common Core State Standards: Upper Elementary English

The following are the reading literature standards addressed for the upper elementary grades. I have listed the Grades 4 and 5 reading standards separately because the language is slightly different. In contrast, the Grades 4 and 5 writing standards appear together as the language is almost identical.

Grades 4–5 Reading Literature Standards Addressed

RL.4.1	Refer to details and examples in a text when explaining what the text says explicitly and when drawing inferences from the text.	RL.5.1	Quote accurately from a text when explaining what the text says explicitly and when drawing inferences from the text.
RL.4.2	Determine a theme of a story, drama, or poem from details in the text; summarize the text.	RL.5.2	Determine a theme of a story, drama, or poem from details in the text, including how characters in a story or drama respond to challenges or how the speaker in a poem reflects upon a topic; summarize the text.

RL.4.7	Make connections between the text of a story or drama and a visual or oral presentation of the text, identifying where each version reflects specific descriptions and directions in the text.	RL.5.7	Analyze how visual and multimedia elements contribute to the meaning, tone, or beauty of a text.

Grades 4–5 Writing Standards Addressed

W.4-5.1	Write opinion pieces on topics or texts, supporting a point of view with reasons and information.
W.4-5.2	Write informative/explanatory texts to examine a topic and convey ideas and information clearly.
W.4-5.4	Produce clear and coherent writing in which the development and organization are appropriate to task, purpose, and audience.
W.4-5.6	With some guidance and support from adults, use technology, including the Internet, to produce and publish writing as well as to interact and collaborate with others.
W.4-5.9	Draw evidence from literary or informational texts to support analysis, reflection, and research.

Note: The language describing each standard is taken directly from the Common Core State Standards Initiative website: www.corestandards.org.

The upper elementary reading standards ask students to reference details and examples from texts, identify central themes, and discuss characters, events, and settings in a story. This requires that students are able to comprehend, summarize, and think critically about what they read.

Three types of writing are required in upper elementary: opinion, informative/explanatory, and narrative. Students must be able to introduce a topic clearly and support that topic with evidence and a clear explanation. Writing should be organized, developed, and "appropriate to task, purpose, and audience" (Standards W.4-5.4). Technology should also be used to "produce and publish" writing (Standards W.4-5.6).

Example Online Activity 6.1. What Does Minli Learn About Greed in the Book *Where the Mountain Meets the Moon* by Grace Lin?

What does Minli learn about greed in the book "Where the Mountain Meets the Moon" by Grace Lin?

Popularity: 0
Vote
Comment

Posted By C. Tucker Moderator to Upper Elementary on 11/10/2011

Greed is a central idea/theme in this book. Choose <u>one</u> moment from the book where you think Minli learns a lesson about greed. Explain what happens and what Minli learns about greed.

How does Minli respond to these moments when she is faced with greed? What does the reader learn about Minli's character and values? How do these moments impact her growth as a character? Use a specific example or a quote from the book to support your answer.

Suggest your own answer or vote for an answer. If you vote for another person's answer, then reply to that person explaining why you agree with them and build on their ideas.

Liland, Stein. "A Fairytale Scene." Mountain. Flickr. 23 Jun 2009. 10 Nov 2011 http://www.flickr.com/photos /53609194@N00/3653694957/.>;;;;

Attachments

Be the first to submit an answer

B　*I*　U̲　S̶　X₂　X²　Ω　⁹⁸　☰　☰　☰　☰　☰　☰　☰　☰

Post

☐ View and Comment (0)　◉ Watch　📄 Topic Library　　　　Action　--Choose--　⬍

Common Core Standards

RL.5.1, RL.5.2, W.4-5.2, W.4-5.4, W.4-5.6, W.4-5.9

This question asks students to consider the theme of greed in Grace Lin's book *Where the Mountain Meets the Moon*. When introducing abstract concepts like theme to younger students, it is helpful to first identify a theme and ask students to discuss it. The next step in a gradual approach to teaching students about theme is to identify a few themes in a given novel and have students select one to discuss in depth. Teachers can also ask students to argue which theme they believe is most important; this can create a lively dialogue about the ideas in literature. Students learn that multiple themes are present in a given text. They also learn to analyze each theme's degree of importance—a skill they will need as they progress through high school. Once they have a clear understanding of what a theme is, then they can begin to identify themes on their own.

This question also asks that students produce a short informative piece of writing that conveys their ideas about what Minli learns about greed in the novel. This requires that they develop their ideas with examples from the novel and analysis of those concrete details.

Weave Online Work Into the Classroom With Student-Centered Activities

1. *Creative Assignment.* Ask students, in groups, to create a collage of images that they believe represent the theme of greed. They can create their collages with magazines, scissors, and glue or use Glogster to create and share a multimedia collage online.

Students love collages, and they can be used as inspiration for an original poem or story about the theme of greed.

Glogster

edu.glogster.com

Create and share multimedia posters online.

Single Free	Teacher Light	Teacher Premium	School Premium
Single license Limited features	Single license 50 students	Single license 200 students	Multilicense 2,500 students
	$29.95 per year	$99 per year	$2 per student per year

2. *Written Reflection and/or Group Discussion.* Ask students to reflect on a time in their lives when they acted greedily or encountered greed in another person.

- What caused the greed?
- How did they respond in this situation?
- What did they learn from this experience?
- Was their greed justified?

Give students time to reflect in writing, then come together as a group to discuss.

3. *Copy Change Poetry-Writing Activity.* Use John Mullan's poem "Greed" to create a copy change poem students can then fill in to make their own. This is a great way to support younger writers in poetry writing. Once students have written their poems, they can publish them by reading them to their group or by posting them online.

"Greed"

by John Mullan

Be wary of Greed. It's _____

that sneaks up _____

It starts with "_____ "

and ends with "_____ "

At first _____ it has an _____

An equal share _____ , but _____

So don't _____

Because _____

Greed will _____ .

Example Online Activity 6.2.
Do You Prefer Reading "Casey at the Bat"
or Listening to a Dramatic Reading of the Poem?

Do you prefer reading "Casey at the Bat" or listening to the dramatic reading of the poem?

Popularity: 0
Vote
Comment

Posted By C. Tucker Moderator to Upper Elementary on 11/10/2011

Read this poem then listen to the dramatic reading by James Earl Jones. Which did you enjoy more?

Compare and contrast the experience of reading versus listening to a dramatic reading of the poem. How did the audio version impact your understanding of the poem itself? Did it add to or take away from the beauty of the poem?

Once you have posted your response, reply thoughtfully to at least two of your classmates. Compliment strong points made, ask questions if something is unclear, and/or build on the ideas shared.

Spenna99. "Casey At The Bat - James Earl Jones." Online video clip. YouTube. 12 Feb 2010. 10 Nov 2011 http://www.youtube.com/watch?v=X-21XQQcXb8.

Attachments

James Earl Jones reads

Casey At The Bat - James Earl Jones

○ I liked reading the poem to myself.

○ I liked listening to the dramatic reading of the poem.

🗨 View and Comment (0)   ◉ Watch

Teacher's Note: You can insert the poem into the description of the question or provide a hyperlink. The poem can be found at the Baseball Almanac website: www.baseball-almanac.com/poetry/po_case.shtml.

Common Core Standards

RL.4-5.7, W.4-5.1, W.4-5.4, W.4-5.6, W.4-5.9

In addition to identifying and discussing key elements of a story, poem, or drama, the Standards ask students to analyze how media impacts the "meaning, tone, or beauty of a text" (Standard RL.5.7). This requires that they think critically about the impact of media.

This question asks students to compare reading a poem with the experience of listening to the dramatic reading to evaluate how the addition of media affects their comprehension and enjoyment of the poem.

In addition to motivating students to think deeply about media and literature, this strategy of pairing literature in the written form with an audio version also makes it easier for a teacher to differentiate instruction for lower-level students and/or second language learners who might struggle with the vocabulary in a given text. Many students—both native speakers and second language learners—exhaust so much energy decoding words that they are not able to focus on understanding the meaning of the words themselves. Listening to a dramatic reading provides clues about the connotation of words and phrases that aid comprehension. This question allows students to benefit from both the visual text and the auditory reading to improve overall comprehension.

Weave Online Work Into the Classroom With Student-Centered Activities

1. *Follow-Up Discussion.* Put the results of this multiple-choice question on the board in the form of a chart showing what percentage of the class said they preferred to read the poem versus listen to it. Use this to motivate a follow-up discussion about the impact of media.

Here are some possible discussion questions:

- How did the poem change when you heard it read aloud?
- Were the emotions you experienced when reading the poem different from those you experienced when listening to the dramatic reading?
- Did you enjoy the reader, James Earl Jones? Why or why not?
- Did the reader add to or distract from the poem?
- Do you think the reading changed the meaning of the poem or the points of emphasis in the poem? Explain.
- Did you struggle with the poem when you read it by yourself? If so, was it easier to understand when you listened to the audio version?

2. *Poetry Assignment.* Ask students to write a poem about a sport or activity they love. *Example Poetry Prompt:* Think about a sport, hobby,

or activity you enjoy—similar to baseball in "Casey at the Bat." Brainstorm possible successes or failures associated with this activity, like hitting a home run or striking out in a baseball game. Then choose one success or failure to be the climactic moment in your poem. As you write your poem, consider elements of poetry: rhyme, repetition, simile, and stanzas. Try to incorporate these elements into your poem.

Publish these poems by sharing them with the class or use a creative online storytelling tool like Storybird to create an online storybook pairing their poetry with images and artwork.

Storybird

storybird.com/teachers

Create art-inspired stories to share, read or print.

Forever Free	**Pro**	**Pro+**
Up to 75 students	Up to 150 students	Up to 300 students
3 classes	Unlimited classes	Unlimited classes
Unlimited Storybirds	Unlimited Storybirds	Unlimited Storybirds
Free	$69 per year	$99 per year

---

3. *Practice Dramatic Readings.* Divide the class into groups or pairs, provide them with poetry, and give them time to practice performing a dramatic reading of their poems. Students should give each other constructive feedback on their dramatic readings. This activity gives students an opportunity to work hands-on with poetry. They must think about the way reading a poem—emphasis of words/phrases, tone of voice, dramatic pauses, and volume—can affect the meaning, tone, or beauty of that poem. Performing a dramatic reading also requires students to have a thorough understanding of the meaning and emotions of the text.

Using an online tool like Blabberize is a fun and less-intimidating approach to a dramatic reading. Students can

Blabberize

blabberize.com

Animate any image and make it talk.

Free

upload a picture (of themselves, a famous historical figure, an object, or an animal), then animate that photo with a recording of their dramatic reading.

Common Core State Standards: Middle School English

The following are the reading literature standards addressed for middle school. The Grades 6, 7, and 8 reading standards are listed separately because the language is slightly different. In contrast, the writing standards for these grades appear together as the language is almost identical.

Grades 6–8 Reading Literature Standards Addressed

RL.6.1	Cite textual evidence to support analysis of what the text says explicitly as well as inferences drawn from the text.	RL.7.1	Cite several pieces of textual evidence to support analysis of what the text says explicitly as well as inferences drawn from the text.	RL.8.1	Cite the textual evidence that most strongly supports an analysis of what the text says explicitly as well as inferences drawn from the text.
RL.6.2	Determine a theme or central idea of a text and how it is conveyed through particular details; provide a summary of the text distinct from personal opinions or judgments.	RL.7.2	Determine a theme or central idea of a text and analyze its development over the course of the text; provide an objective summary of the text.	RL.8.2	Determine a theme or central idea of a text and analyze its development over the course of the text, including its relationship to the characters, setting, and plot; provide an objective summary of the text.

Grades 6–8 Writing Standards Addressed

W.6-8.1	Write opinion pieces on topics or texts, supporting a point of view with reasons and information.
W.6-8.2	Write informative/explanatory texts to examine a topic and convey ideas and information clearly.
W.6-8.4	Produce clear and coherent writing in which the development and organization are appropriate to task, purpose, and audience.
W.6-8.6	Use technology, including the Internet, to produce and publish writing as well as to interact and collaborate with others.
W.6-8.9	Draw evidence from literary or informational texts to support analysis, reflection, and research.

Note: The language describing each standard is taken directly from the Common Core State Standards Initiative website: www.corestandards.org.

The reading standards in middle school move students from identifying and explaining to analyzing and making inferences. Students must begin to think critically about characters, events, themes, story elements, and lines of dialogue. They must compare and contrast the written text with other representations of that same text in different mediums using analysis to support their comparisons. The focus transitions from comprehension and explanation to critical thinking and analysis.

In middle school, opinion pieces develop into argument writing, which is slightly different from persuasive writing. Argument writing convinces "the audience with the perceived merit and reasonableness of the claims and proof offered" (Owens, 2011, para. 1). In contrast, persuasive writing attempts to "persuade using . . . 'the emotions the writer evokes in the audience'" (para. 1). The emphasis in argument writing is to present a logical argument that is supported by strong evidence. In addition to argument/opinion writing, informative/explanatory and narrative writing continue to be emphasized in the standards for middle school.

Example Online Activity 6.3. *Roll of Thunder, Hear My Cry:* Do You Think the Boycott of the Wallace's Store Was the Best Way for the African American Community to Fight Racism?

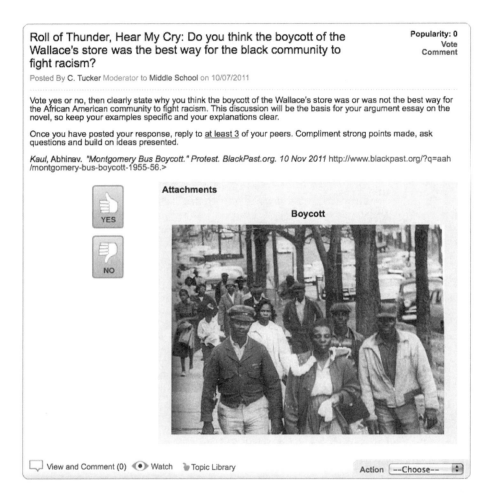

Roll of Thunder, Hear My Cry: Do you think the boycott of the Wallace's store was the best way for the black community to fight racism?

Popularity: 0
Vote
Comment

Posted By C. Tucker Moderator to **Middle School** on 10/07/2011

Vote yes or no, then clearly state why you think the boycott of the Wallace's store was or was not the best way for the African American community to fight racism. This discussion will be the basis for your argument essay on the novel, so keep your examples specific and your explanations clear.

Once you have posted your response, reply to <u>at least 3</u> of your peers. Compliment strong points made, ask questions and build on ideas presented.

Kaul, Abhinav. "Montgomery Bus Boycott." Protest. BlackPast.org. 10 Nov 2011 http://www.blackpast.org/?q=aah /montgomery-bus-boycott-1955-56.>

YES

NO

Attachments

Boycott

View and Comment (0)   Watch   Topic Library   Action [--Choose--]

Common Core Standards

RL.6-8.1, W.6-8.1, W.6-8.4, W.6-8.6, W.6-8.9

This yes-or-no discussion question is the first step in writing an argument essay. It is helpful for middle school students to have the time and space to articulate an argument, explain and support their position, and engage in a discussion about their position prior to writing an essay. Students may initially feel they have a strong argument; however, they can learn a great deal from reading their peers' perspectives. Often they will hear a point of view or argument they had not considered. This provides them with possible counterarguments that need to be addressed in their essays.

Beginning an argument essay with a debate-style discussion question online not only creates interest but also teaches the importance of backing up statements with strong evidence. Students identify areas of weakness and highlight them in an online debate or discussion. This challenges members of the class to carefully select moments from the text and quotes that are strong enough to justify their position on an issue. This translates into stronger concrete details and more thorough analysis of those details in the actual essay.

Weave Online Work Into the Classroom With Student-Centered Activities

1. *Creative Research Project.* Assign groups of students an important historical figure from the civil rights movement to research.

- Dr. Martin Luther King Jr.
- Rosa Parks
- Malcolm X
- Andrew Goodman

> **Wix**
>
> www.wix.com
>
> Create a flash website. Drag and drop images and information without programming.
>
> Free

Students then create an informational poster to present to the class or design an informational website using Wix to teach others about this important figure and his or her impact on history.

2. *Timeline Research Activity.* Divide the class into groups and assign each group a topic to research.

- Jim Crow laws
- Harlem Renaissance
- Formation of the NAACP
- Separate but equal
- Scottsboro trial

Then have each group collaborate to create a timeline detailing the key events and people related to this topic. Students can use Tiki-Toki to create an interactive multimedia timeline of their topic, incorporating text, images, and video. *Note:* If a group of students work together on a single Tiki-Toki timeline, a teacher can save money because a fewer number of timelines will be needed.

Tiki-Toki

www.tiki-toki.com

Create a Web-based multimedia timeline.

Free	Bronze Account	Silver Account	Education Account
1 free timeline No group edits	5 timelines per month Group edit capability	25 timelines per month Group edit capability	Teacher gets a Silver Account, and up to 50 students get a Bronze Account
	$5 per month	$20 per month	$100 per year

Teacher's Note: The Rise and Fall of Jim Crow website (www.pbs.org/wnet/jimcrow/) has information about the Jim Crow laws, the formation of the NAACP, and the birth of the civil rights movement.

Read, Write, Think

www.readwritethink.org/classroom-resources/student-interactives/venn-diagram-circles-30006.html

Create a variety of Venn diagrams online.

Free

History.com

www.history.com/topics/civil-rights-movement

Access a wide variety of photos, videos, articles, speeches, and primary and secondary sources.

Free

3. *Group Research and Venn Diagram Activity.* Have students research the Montgomery Bus Boycott and then compare it to the boycott in the novel. How were they similar? How were they different? What inspired each? How did each end? What did each accomplish? Students create a Venn diagram that clearly identifies their main points.

Teacher's Note: The Montgomery Advertiser hosts a site (montgomeryboycott.com) that has news articles, biographies, information on

Rosa Parks, and a timeline of events. History.com also has information on the Civil Rights Movement, including the Montgomery Bus Boycott and the March on Washington.

Example Online Activity 6.4. *The Adventures of Tom Sawyer:* How Does Guilt Motivate Action in the Novel?

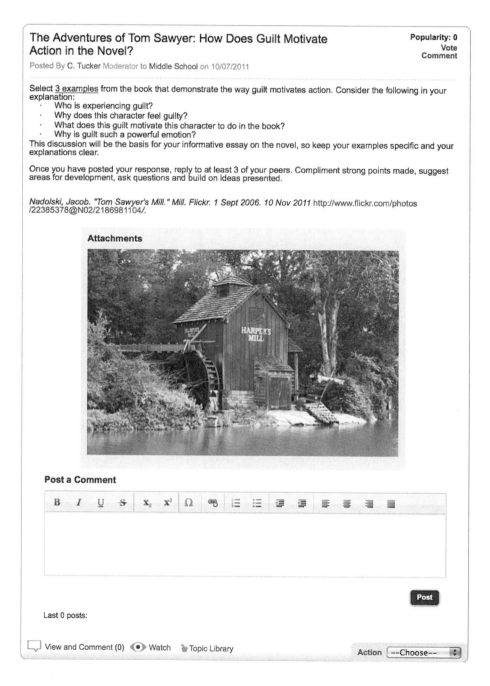

The Adventures of Tom Sawyer: How Does Guilt Motivate Action in the Novel?

Popularity: 0
Vote
Comment

Posted By C. Tucker Moderator to Middle School on 10/07/2011

Select 3 examples from the book that demonstrate the way guilt motivates action. Consider the following in your explanation:
· Who is experiencing guilt?
· Why does this character feel guilty?
· What does this guilt motivate this character to do in the book?
· Why is guilt such a powerful emotion?
This discussion will be the basis for your informative essay on the novel, so keep your examples specific and your explanations clear.

Once you have posted your response, reply to at least 3 of your peers. Compliment strong points made, suggest areas for development, ask questions and build on ideas presented.

Nadolski, Jacob. "Tom Sawyer's Mill." Mill. Flickr. 1 Sept 2006. 10 Nov 2011 http://www.flickr.com/photos/22385378@N02/2186981104/.

Attachments

Post a Comment

B   *I*   U   S   x₂   x²   Ω   ∞   ≡   ≡   ≡   ≡   ≡   ≡   ≡   ≡

Post

Last 0 posts:

View and Comment (0)   Watch   Topic Library   Action --Choose--

Common Core Standards

RL.6-8.1, RL.6-8.2, W.6-8.2, W.6-8.4, W.6-8.6, W.6-8.9

Informative/explanatory writing in middle school requires that students be able to "examine a topic and convey ideas, concepts, and information through the selection" (Standards W.6-8.2). Instead of focusing on a single moment or section of the text to discuss and explain, students must be able to write about the topic in the context of the entire piece of literature. The scope of writing is much larger, yet the writing must stay clear, focused, and concise. The topic must be developed with "relevant, well-chosen facts, definitions, concrete details, quotations" (Standards W.6-8.2). Instead of relying solely on summarized examples, the textual evidence and subsequent analysis of that evidence must be more specific.

This question asks students to consider the theme of guilt and how that emotion motivates action in the novel. Instead of focusing on a particular section of the novel, students must think about the entire work of literature. They have to identify three moments from the novel when they believe guilt motivates action. This ties together the reading standards and the writing standards in a single task; students must analyze a central theme and use it to write a clear informative piece of writing.

Weave Online Work Into the Classroom With Student-Centered Activities

1. *Written Reflection.* Ask students to think of a time in their lives when they were motivated by guilt. Have them write about it and then share in groups.

- What did they do that caused them to experience guilt?
- How did feeling guilty motivate them?
- Did the guilt they experienced keep them from making similar mistakes in the future?

These reflective writing assignments can also be done using an online journal, like Penzu (for more on Penzu, see p. 119). Online journal entries can be shared, locked, or printed, allowing students to keep their reflective writing in one location throughout the school year.

2. *Group Discussion.* Divide the class into small groups, and ask them to discuss the following questions.

- Does Huck ever experience guilt in the novel? If so, when? How does he respond to guilt? If not, why not?
- How does Huck respond to Tom's feelings of guilt?
- How are Tom and Huck different in terms of their values and morals?
- How did Huck's childhood impact his feelings about right and wrong?

Once students have discussed these questions, have them use their ideas to create a Venn diagram comparing Huck and Tom.

3. *Artistic Activity.* Have students create a comic strip visually representing an important scene from the novel involving both Tom and Huck. The comic strip should reveal aspects of their personalities and focus on a central theme in the novel. Students can draw their own comics by hand or use an online comic maker tool like Pixton.

Pixton

pixton.com/schools

Create a comic online. Design your own characters, upload pictures, add sound, use a variety of speech bubbles, then print, download, or embed.

30-day free trial with 50 students

Pricing for educators depends on number of students and amount of time needed.

Common Core State Standards: High School English

The following are the reading literature standards addressed for the high school level. The Grades 9–10 and 11–12 reading standards are listed separately because the language is slightly different. In contrast, the writing standards for all four grades appear together as the language is almost identical.

Grades 9–12 Reading Literature Standards Addressed

RL.9-10.1	Cite strong and thorough textual evidence to support analysis of what the text says explicitly as well as inferences drawn from the text.	RL.11-12.1	Cite strong and thorough textual evidence to support analysis of what the text says explicitly as well as inferences drawn from the text, including determining where the text leaves matters uncertain.
RL.9-10.7	Analyze the representation of a subject or a key scene in two different artistic mediums, including what is emphasized or absent in each treatment.	RL.11-12.7	Analyze multiple interpretations of a story, drama, or poem (e.g., recorded or live production of a play or recorded novel or poetry), evaluating how each version interprets the source text.

Grades 9–12 Writing Standards Addressed

W.9-12.2	Write informative/explanatory texts to examine and convey complex ideas, concepts, and information clearly and accurately through the effective selection, organization, and analysis of content.
W.9-12.4	Produce clear and coherent writing in which the development, organization, and style are appropriate to task, purpose, and audience.
W.9-12.6	Use technology, including the Internet, to produce, publish, and update individual or shared writing products, taking advantage of technology's capacity to link to other information and to display information flexibly and dynamically.
W.9-12.9	Draw evidence from literary or informational texts to support analysis, reflection, and research.

Note: The language describing each standard is taken directly from the Common Core State Standards Initiative website: www.corestandards.org.

At the high school level, students should be able to use strong textual evidence to support both the explicit and implicit meaning of a given text. Students must be able to make inferences based on the information available and identify areas of ambiguity in the text.

They must move from simply identifying and discussing a central idea to analyzing how multiple themes in a given work "interact and build on one another" (Standards RI.11-12.2). Attention to an author's use of diction, syntax, and figurative language is also emphasized at this level. Students need to demonstrate an understanding of how language can be used to create meaning and achieve a particular tone. Beyond the language, students must also think critically about how the author has chosen to order events in a text.

High school builds on the same writing requirements established in middle school. Argument/opinion, informative/explanatory, and narrative writing are identified specifically in the Standards. Even though the types of writing required are the same, "students should demonstrate increasing sophistication in all aspects of language use, from vocabulary and syntax to the development and organization of ideas, and they should address increasingly demanding content and sources" (Writing Standards: Introduction).

Example Online Activity 6.5. *A Raisin in the Sun:* What a Difference a Film Can Make!

Common Core Standards

RL.9-10.1, RL.9-10.7, RL.11-12.1, RL.11-12.7, W.9-12.4, W.9-12.6, W.9-12.9

This discussion question asks students to evaluate different movie versions of the play *A Raisin in the Sun* and analyze the way that the different versions interpret the same text. Students are inundated by media, so it is important that they think critically about that media. This question asks them to consider how a director's decisions, casting, and set design can impact the overall effect of the performance.

Teacher's Note: The video clip from the 1961 film version of *A Raisin in the Sun* used in this question can be found on YouTube.

Weave Online Work Into the Classroom With Student-Centered Activities

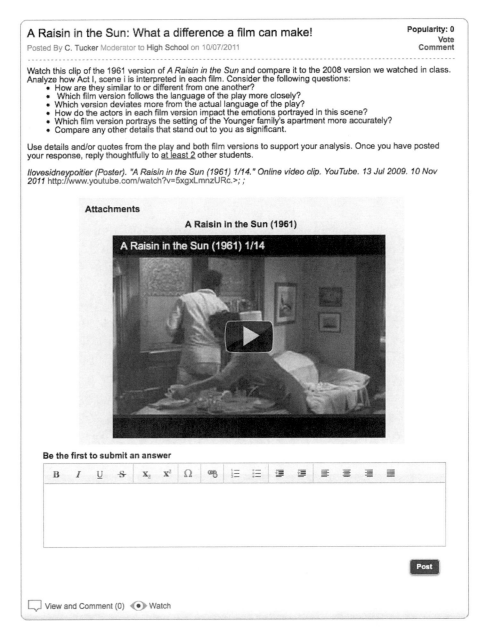

1. *Acting.* Assign roles to small acting groups for subsequent scenes from the play. Give students time to read their roles and practice performing the scenes in their acting groups. Then have them perform their scenes for the class. As a class, discuss the way acting helps to reinforce students' understanding of each scene.

Groups can take photos and video clips of their scenes using mobile devices in the classroom and then use these to create an Animoto video.

Animoto

www.animoto.com

This online video-making tool enables students to pair photos and short videos with music to create a high-quality video that can be shared. Students can choose from a collection of images, video clips, and music or upload their own.

Lite	Plus	Pro
Unlimited 30-second videos	Unlimited feature-length films	Unlimited feature-length films
		Themed video styles plus exclusive pro video styles
Themed video styles	Themed video styles	1,100+ tracks of music
		HD upgrades included
600+ tracks of music	600+ tracks of music	Download to computer and DVD
Free	$5 per month	$39 per month

2. *Soundtrack Project.* Students select a song to pair with each scene of the play and explain their choice in writing. How does the song match the scene in terms of themes, action, characters, and/or pacing? Students can do this individually or collaboratively in pairs or groups, then discuss their choices.

This can also be facilitated as an ongoing online project in which students post their song selection and analysis each night after they complete a scene. During my Shakespeare units—*Othello* and *Romeo and Juliet*—I have students select a song for every scene of the play, then post their song and analysis online. I highlight some of the strongest selections and play the songs associated with them (when I can find them online) the next day in class. It is a fun way to get students connecting with literature using music—something they are passionate about.

3. *Rewrite the Last Scene.* In writing groups, ask students to rewrite the last scene of *A Raisin in the Sun* with character lines and stage directions. Groups can act out or film their rewritten final scene to share with the class. Videos could be edited and paired with music online using iMovie or Movie Maker and then shared on a video-hosting site like SchoolTube or YouTube Education.

Example Online Activity 6.6. *Fahrenheit 451: Transition From Reading to Burning . . .*

Fahrenheit 451: Analyze the Transition from Reading to Burning...

Posted By C. Tucker in English to High School on 1/3/2011

Popularity: 0
Vote
Comment

Choose <u>one</u> of the factors below that contributed to the transition from valuing books to burning them. Begin by clearly stating the factor you are focusing on then develop your analysis of the effect of this factor on society.

How did the factor you chose impact the role of literature in people's lives? Why were books, literature and knowledge in general devalued? Support your statements with quotes from the text.

Pcorreia. "Book Burning." Burning. Flickr. 12 May 2007. 10 Nov 2011 http://www.flickr.com/photos/70458860@N00/517900257/.>;

Attachments

○ Advances in Technology

○ Population Growth

○ Speed of Life Increasing

○ Shortened School Day

○ Pursuit of Pleasure

○ Increased Physical Activity/Organized Sports

○ Minority Pressure/Fear of Offending

▢ View and Comment (0)   ◄ ■ ► Watch

Common Core Standards

RL.9-12.1, W.9-12.2, W.9-12.4, W.9-12.6, W.9-12.9

This question asks that students focus on one factor that is responsible for the transition from reading books to burning them in Bradbury's novel. The sequence of events and multitude of factors identified in the novel are often confusing for students who struggle to understand the subtle ways these factors overlapped and influenced society's changing views on literature and education. This question simplifies the task of understanding this complex shift by asking students to focus on a single factor. Then they can read what their peers have said and benefit from all the ideas shared. This results in a better understanding of the factors at work, making it possible for students to draw inferences based on the text. Ultimately, they work as a group to put the pieces together to understand how Bradbury's society evolved.

Weave Online Work Into the Classroom With Student-Centered Activities

1. *Create a Flowchart.* Ask small groups of students to use what they learned about the transition from reading to burning in Bradbury's futuristic society to create a flowchart of events that show this progression. They should work as a group to create 8–10 images that represent

Gliffy

www.gliffy.com

Gliffy is a collaborative tool that students can use to design and create high-quality flowcharts and diagrams together.

Free

the changes that took place. Pairing the images with quotes from the text can make this activity a bit more challenging for advanced students. Students can draw their flowcharts on construction paper to be posted around the room, or they can use Gliffy, a collaborative online flowchart tool.

2. *Debate.* Could this transition from reading books to burning them happen in our society? Break the class into two groups to debate this topic.

3. *Research.* Ask groups of students to research an example of book burning from history. Select either the Cultural Revolution in China

when Mao Zedong burned books or the Holocaust in Europe when Hitler burned books. Then discuss:

- What types of books were burned?
- Why were they burned?
- Who did the burning?
- What was the impact on society?
- How did the population at large react to this?

Students can design an informational poster, using Glogster (for more on Glogster, see p. 93), or the website Wix (for more on Wix, see p. 101).

Chapter Summary

The Standards for English Language Arts are broken into two categories: reading and writing. Because the Standards build on the skills taught in the previous year, it is important that students be able to demonstrate competency at the end of each academic year.

The reading standards stress frequency and variety; students should read often from a wide range of texts. Teachers using an online learning platform or learning management system can make an array of texts more accessible by embedding documents—stories, articles, poetry, and biographies. Engaging students in online discussions about the literature they are reading encourages them to employ higher-order thinking to analyze, synthesize, and evaluate what they read.

Online discussions and group work also require that students articulate their ideas in writing, which addresses the writing standards as well. Learning to communicate thoughts clearly and concisely takes practice. If online conversations and group work are part of the curriculum, students constantly fine-tune their writing to produce clear and coherent work.

The writing standards specifically focus on three types of writing: argument/opinion, informative/explanatory, and narrative. Argument/opinion writing must make a clear claim, then support that claim with strong evidence and analysis. Informative/explanatory writing examines and explains complex ideas through the use of concrete examples and analysis. Finally, narrative writing develops real or imagined events, situations, or experiences while effectively using language and narrative techniques to develop this type of writing.

This chapter provides examples of online discussion questions, topics, and writing prompts as well as student-centered classroom activities that require students to satisfy multiple standards at once. Writing is required throughout, but several of the prompts are specifically intended to develop argument/opinion, informative/ explanatory, and narrative writing as described in the Common Core State Standards. Many of these online tasks can be developed into process papers if teachers want to continue to build on the work done online.

Book Study Questions

1. What is the biggest challenge associated with teaching reading? How might you address this challenge using a blended instruction approach to reading, understanding, and analyzing a text? How would the online space help you improve your reading program? How can you encourage your students to read more? Do you believe it will help motivate students to read if you stress how much reading can help them improve their own writing? Brainstorm creative solutions using a blended learning model. For example, consider posting samples of excellent writing online and suggest to students that if they like the samples, they should consider reading the works from which the samples are taken.

2. Do you currently use media in your reading program? If so, what types do you use? How have your students responded to media? Where do you find your media? How does it help you differentiate instruction and appeal to multiple learning styles? Do you have resources you would recommend for quality media for English teachers?

3. How can media support lower-level readers in your class? What kinds of media would make the readings more accessible and less intimidating? What are the benefits of having students listen to a recording or watch a film version in addition to reading a text?

4. What is the biggest challenge you face in teaching students how to write well? How might a blended instruction approach to writing help you address this challenge? How would the online space help improve your writing program? Brainstorm creative solutions using a blended learning model.

5. How would you use the online space to actively engage students in peer editing? What strategies would you use to keep

the peer feedback focused and valuable? What benefits would you expect online peer editing to have on the overall quality of writing?

6. How can using an online learning platform help you scaffold writing assignments so they better support all students in reaching grade-level proficiency in writing? Think about a writing assignment you currently use with students—how could you use the online space to better support students during the different parts of the writing process?

7. How can the online space be leveraged to create more effective writing groups to provide a support network as students write? How many students do you think you would ideally have in each writing group? How might you group students to ensure that writing groups are successful and productive?

8. How can you use online media tools to allow students to explore digital writing and develop media literacy? Are there online tools you currently use or are interested in using to support students in creating multimedia representations of their writing? For example, would you enjoy having students create an iMovie of an original narrative or use a digital tool like Storybird to transform their story into a digital book with original photographs or artwork? What are the benefits of having students pair media with writing?

Reference

Owens, B. (2011, January 26). Common Core State Standards FAQ #2: Argumentative vs. persuasive writing [Web log]. Retrieved from http:// emcpublishing-mirrorswindows.blogspot.com/2011/01/common-core-state-standards-q-2.html

7

History/Social Studies

The standards are built on an "integrated model of literacy," recognizing that reading and writing are interconnected and should be taught in all subject areas. As a result, the history/social studies standards for kindergarten through fifth grade are included in the English language arts (ELA) standards. The example online discussion questions, writing tasks, and activities in the upper elementary history/social studies section of this chapter reference English language arts standards for fourth and fifth grade.

The standards for Grades 6–12 are split into two sections: English language arts (as discussed in Chapter 6) and literacy in history/social studies, science, and technical studies. "This division reflects the unique, time-honored place of ELA teachers in developing students' literacy skills while at the same time recognizing that teachers in other areas must have a role in this development as well" (English Language Arts Standards: Introduction: Key Design Considerations). For that reason, this chapter provides examples for history and social studies teachers that demonstrate how an online environment can be used to support students in reading, analyzing, and writing about historical figures, events, documents, speeches, and texts. Many of the questions in this history/social studies section require that students meet both reading and writing standards for their grade level.

Common Core State Standards: Upper Elementary History/Social Studies

The following are the reading informational text standards addressed for the upper elementary level. I have used the Grades 4–5 English language arts reading informational text standards and writing standards because the history/social studies standards are integrated into the English standards until sixth grade. The Grades 4–5 writing standards are listed together as the language is almost identical.

Grades 4–5 Reading Information Standards Addressed

RI.4.1	Refer to details and examples in a text when explaining what the text says explicitly and when drawing inferences from the text.	RI.5.1	Quote accurately from a text when explaining what the text says explicitly and when drawing inferences from the text.
RI.4.3	Explain events, procedures, ideas, or concepts in a historical, scientific, or technical text, including what happened and why, based on specific information in the text.	RI.5.3	Explain the relationships or interactions between two or more individuals, events, ideas, or concepts in a historical, scientific, or technical text based on specific information in the text.
RI.4.9	Integrate information from two texts on the same topic in order to write or speak about the subject knowledgeably.	RI.5.7	Draw on information from multiple print or digital sources, demonstrating the ability to locate an answer to a question quickly or to solve a problem efficiently.

Grades 4–5 Writing Standards Addressed

W.4-5.1	Write opinion pieces on topics or texts, supporting a point of view with reasons and information.
W.4-5.2	Write informative/explanatory texts to examine a topic and convey ideas and information clearly.
W.4-5.4	Produce clear and coherent writing in which the development and organization are appropriate to task, purpose, and audience.
W.4-5.6	With some guidance and support from adults, use technology, including the Internet, to produce and publish writing as well as to interact and collaborate with others.
W.4-5.7	Conduct short research projects that use several sources to build knowledge through investigation of different aspects of a topic.
W.4-5.9	Draw evidence from literary or informational texts to support analysis, reflection, and research.

Note: The language describing each standard is taken directly from the Common Core State Standards Initiative website: www.corestandards.org.

I have used the reading standards for informational texts and the writing standards for K–5 as a guide for the activities in this section, because the "standards for K–5 reading in history/social studies . . . are integrated into the K–5 Reading standards" (English Language Arts Standards: History/Social Studies: Introduction).

Students in fourth and fifth grade are expected to read informational texts and quote accurately to clearly support explanations and draw reasonable conclusions from information. As they read, students must be able to identify and discuss key ideas in a text and "explain the relationships . . . between two or more individuals, events, ideas, or concepts" (Standard RI.5.3). The focus is comprehension and explanation with attempts at analysis.

The writing standards for K–5 focus on opinion and informational writing. Writing should contain narrative elements, but the focus of writing at this level is to introduce a topic and support that topic with evidence and a clear explanation. Writing should be organized, developed, and "appropriate to task, purpose, and audience" (Standard W.4-5.4). Technology should also be used to produce and publish writing.

Example Online Activity 7.1.
Early United States History:
Research Pre-Columbian Settlements

Early United States History: Researching Pre-Columbian
Settlements

Popularity: 0
Vote
Comment

Select <u>one</u> of the pre-Columbian settlements listed below to research and discuss. Consider the following questions as you research:

- How did geography impact their way of life?
- What was their diet like? Did they hunt, gather, farm, or fish?
- Describe their customs and/or traditions.
- What type of economic system and/or government did they have?
- Compare and contrast the role of men and women in this settlement.
- What challenges did they face prior to the arrival of the Europeans?
- How was this settlement impacted by the arrival of the Europeans?

Include quotes and/or factual information from <u>at least 2</u> reliable online sources in your answer.

Once you have posted your description complete with research, reply thoughtfully to <u>at least 2</u> other students. Compliment strong points, ask questions, suggest facts that would improve their explanation and build on ideas shared!

Mickeyvdo. "Warrior." Native American. Flickr. 8 Apr 2011. 12 Jan 2012.
http://www.flickr.com/photos/38159452@N04/5611832033/

Attachments

Warrior

○ American Indians of Pacific Northwest

○ Nomadic nations of Great Plains

○ Woodland people east of the Mississippi River

○ Pueblo people in the desert Southwest

○ Cliff dwellers

🗩 View and Comment (0) ◉ Watch

Common Core Standards

RI.4-5.4, RI.5.7, W.4-5.2, W.4-5.4, W.4-5.6, W.4-5.9

This activity asks students to research specific indigenous settlements that existed prior to Columbus's landing in the New World. Students must select a settlement to research; describe the lifestyle, diet, economy, and culture of this group; and evaluate the impact of the European conquest of America on these indigenous people. This combines research, critical thinking about online resources, analysis, and informative writing.

Weave Online Work Into the Classroom With Student-Centered Activities

1. *Dear Diary.* Assign each student a role in the settlement they researched (e.g., mother, father, young man or woman, chief, warrior, child, healer). Ask them to reflect on what that person's daily life would have been like in that settlement. Then have them write two diary entries from that person's perspective. The first entry should be written before the arrival of the Europeans, revealing information about their family relationships, culture, responsibilities, fears, and hopes. The second entry should be written after the Europeans arrived, detailing the changes that have taken place as a result of their arrival.

These diary entries should be written in first person and must include sensory details and factual information learned during the students' research and online discussions.

Students can use Penzu to create an online journal where they can type their work, upload photos, and lock some journal entries while sharing others. The ability to lock and share writing makes it possible for students to have an online journal for both their personal and academic entries.

2. *Family Customs.* After students research the customs and traditions of a pre-Columbian settlement, ask them to

Penzu

penzu.com

Create your own personal online diary or journal. Students can write, insert photos, print, share, or lock.

Free

Photovisi

www.photovisi.com

Make customizable photo collages online that can be downloaded and printed.

Free

think about the customs and traditions that are unique to their culture and/or family. Have students create a collage that reflects a family custom. Students can create their collages using magazine cutouts and pictures or a free online photo collage tool, like Photovisi (see p.119).

3. *Reporting Back Home.* Ask students to imagine they are priests traveling with Columbus and his men on their voyage to the New World. As literate members of the crew, they have been asked to write reports back to King Ferdinand and Queen Isabella. Their reports should include detailed impressions of the Native Americans and the land.

Teacher's Note: It might be valuable to provide students with an excerpt from Bartolome Ke Las Casas's *A Short Account of the Destruction of the Indies,* which is available at www.thelatinlibrary .com/imperialism/readings/casas.html.

Example Online Activity 7.2. Boston Massacre: Should This Event Be Called a Massacre?

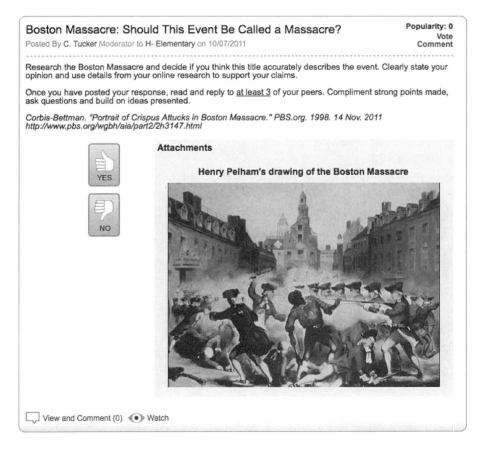

Boston Massacre: Should This Event Be Called a Massacre?

Popularity: 0
Vote
Comment

Posted By C. Tucker Moderator to H- Elementary on 10/07/2011

Research the Boston Massacre and decide if you think this title accurately describes the event. Clearly state your opinion and use details from your online research to support your claims.

Once you have posted your response, read and reply to at least 3 of your peers. Compliment strong points made, ask questions and build on ideas presented.

Corbis-Bettman. "Portrait of Crispus Attucks in Boston Massacre." PBS.org. 1998. 14 Nov. 2011 http://www.pbs.org/wgbh/aia/part2/2h3147.html

YES

NO

Attachments

Henry Pelham's drawing of the Boston Massacre

View and Comment (0)   Watch

Common Core Standards

RI.5.6, RI.5.7, W.4-5.1, W.4-5.4, W.4-5.6, W.4-5.7, W 4-5.9

Students must research a moment in history, then identify bias in the historical account and/or representation of the event. Instead of believing everything they read, this question encourages students to question the validity of what they read online or even in a textbook. This conversation highlights the way bias has shaped how people think about particular historical figures and events. Students have to form an opinion and justify their position. This is also an introduction to argument writing, which is required in Grades 6–12.

Weave Online Work Into the Classroom With Student-Centered Activities

1. *Comparing Primary and Secondary Sources.* In small groups, students read a primary and secondary account of the Boston Massacre.

- Identify the perspective that each account is written from. Are there any possible biases present?
- Which account do you think is more reliable?
- How are the two stories different?
- Why do you think these differences exist?
- What might the differences in the accounts tell us about what actually happened?

> **History.com**
>
> www.history.com
> Great resource for historical information, sources, videos, and photographs.
> Free

Teacher's Note: History.com has a collection of videos about the Boston Massacre: http://tinyurl.com/77kycym

Teacher's Note: History Wiz has eyewitness accounts from both sides of the incident, and History.com is an excellent resource for secondary sources.

> **History Wiz**
>
> www.historywiz.com
> Collection of historical materials and primary sources.
> Free

2. *Group Problem-Solving Activity.* Divide the class into groups, and have them design a strategy for how the Boston Massacre could have been avoided.

- How could the conflict that led to the Boston Massacre have been resolved without violence?
- What compromise could have been reached?
- What do you feel would have been the best approach to dealing with this dispute?

Students should clearly outline their plan as a group and be ready to present it to the class.

3. *Reenactment.* Assign students roles to play in a classroom reenactment of the Boston Massacre. Discuss this event in history prior to the reenactment so students understand their role and how to act out their part. Follow this reenactment with a discussion about the event—people involved, motivations, and consequences.

Common Core State Standards: Middle School History/Social Studies

The following are the literacy standards for history/social studies addressed for middle school. The literacy and writing sections of the history/social studies standards combine Grades 6–8 just as they appear below.

Grades 6–8 Literacy in History/Social Studies Standards Addressed

RH.6-8.1	Cite specific textual evidence to support analysis of primary and secondary sources.
RH.6-8.2	Determine the central ideas or information of a primary or secondary source; provide an accurate summary of the source distinct from prior knowledge or opinions.
RH.6-8.4	Determine the meaning of words and phrases as they are used in a text, including vocabulary specific to domains related to history/social studies.
RH.6-8.6	Identify aspects of a text that reveal an author's point of view or purpose (e.g., loaded language, inclusion or avoidance of particular facts).

Grades 6–8 Writing Standards Addressed

WHST.6-8.1	Write arguments focused on *discipline-specific content.*
WHST.6-8.2	Write informative/explanatory texts, including the narration of historical events, scientific procedures/experiments, or technical processes.
WHST.6-8.4	Produce clear and coherent writing in which the development, organization, and style are appropriate to task, purpose, and audience.
WHST.6-8.6	Use technology, including the Internet, to produce and publish writing and present the relationships between information and ideas clearly and efficiently.
WHST.6-8.9	Draw evidence from informational texts to support analysis, reflection, and research.

Note: The language describing each standard is taken directly from the Common Core State Standards Initiative website: www.corestandards.org.

In Grades 6–8 students must read, summarize, and analyze primary and secondary source documents. They should be able to determine the meaning of words and phrases, describe how information is presented, evaluate bias, and discuss the relationship between primary and secondary sources.

Library of Congress

www.loc.gov/teachers

Collection of primary and secondary sources as well as teaching materials.

Free

In addition, students must be able to write both argument and informative pieces focused on discipline-specific content. Using primary and secondary sources as inspiration for these types of writing encourages students to develop their reading and writing skills simultaneously.

Example Online Activity 7.3. Read and Listen to Martin Luther King's "I Have a Dream" Speech: Has King's Dream Come True?

Read and Listen to Martin Luther King's "I Have a Dream" Speech: Has King's Dream Come True?

Popularity: 0
Vote
Comment

Posted By C. Tucker Moderator to H- Middle School on 10/06/2011

Watch the video clip of Martin Luther King delivering his "I Have a Dream" speech at the March on Washington in 1963.

Do you think Dr. King's "dream" has come true? Vote "yes" or "no," clearly state your opinion and provide specific examples to support your position.

Once you have posted your response, reply thoughtfully to at least 2 other students. Compliment strong points, ask questions and build on ideas shared!

Sullentoys (Poster). "Martin Luther King- I Have a Dream- August 28, 1963." Online video clip. YouTube. 20 Jan 2011. 10 Oct 2011 http://www.youtube.com/watch?v=smEqnnklfYs>

Attachments

Martin Luther King

Martin Luther King "I have a dream"

American Rhetoric

www.americanrhetoric.com/speechbank.htm

Database of text, audio, and video speeches, lectures, debates, and interviews.

Free

Teacher's Note: The text of Dr. King's "I Have a Dream" speech can be copied and pasted directly into the online discussion topic, or a hyperlink can be provided. The speech can be found on the American Rhetoric website: www.americanrhetoric.com/speeches/mlkihaveadream.htm.

Common Core Standards

RH.6-8.1, RH.6-8.2, WHST.6-8.2, WHST.6-8.4, WHST.6-8.6, WHST.6-8.9

This question provides students with both the text of Martin Luther King's "I Have a Dream" speech and the video recording of him speaking at the March on Washington. Pairing the text with media makes it easy for teachers to differentiate instruction for students who struggle with reading or language proficiency. The video can be paused or watched several times depending on the students' needs, which puts them in control of their learning pace to better understand the content. Dr. King's powerful voice and oratory skills bring the speech to life and add depth and emotion, making the words more meaningful for students.

Students must read and listen to the speech, form a clear argument, and support their position with details and textual evidence from the speech, their text, and/or online resources. This requires that they think critically about his speech and the current state of race relations in the United States. They must also compare his dream to the current reality. Teachers can add a requirement asking students to include research about current race relations in the United States to support their opinions.

This task combines a critical reading of the text with argument writing and online research. This question can be used as a first step toward a more complete formal argument essay.

Weave Online Work Into the Classroom With Student-Centered Activities

1. *Wordplay in Dr. King's Speech.* Choose 10 key words from Martin Luther King's "I Have a Dream" speech, or create a Wordle using the "I

Wordle
www.wordle.net
Create a colorful word cloud.
Free

have a dream" portion of the speech. Then present the list of words or the Wordle to students. Students should select one word to inspire an acrostic poem, which explores the word's meaning in relation to Dr. King's dream.

2. *Comparing Primary and Secondary Sources.* Provide students with a primary and secondary account of the March on Washington. The primary source should be from an attendee's point of view; the secondary source should be a newspaper article or secondhand account of the event. Ask students to compare the two accounts of the event, analyzing the similarities and differences. Students discuss in small groups and then as a class.

- Identify the perspective that each account is written from. Are there any possible biases present?
- Which account do you think is more reliable? Why?
- How are the two stories similar and/or different?
- Why do you think these differences exist?
- What might the differences in the accounts tell us about what actually happened?

3. *What's Your Dream for America?* Ask students to reflect on the following questions and articulate their dream in a written reflection. Have them write on their own and then discuss in small groups.

- What is your dream for our country?
- What changes would you like to see in the future?
- What problems exist that you think we need to focus on solving?
- What challenges stand in the way of your dream?
- How can these challenges be overcome?

Lino

en.linoit.com

Online multimedia sticky note board and canvas. Post text, files, photos, and video.

Free

Teachers can extend this activity into a creative and collaborative "Dream Board" project online using Lino. In groups or as a class, students can create a virtual canvas where they post words, phrases, quotes, photos, and videos that represent their dream for this country.

Example Online Activity 7.4. "Blood, Toil, Tears, and Sweat: Address to Parliament on May 13, 1940" by Winston Churchill

"Blood, Toil, Tears and Sweat: Address to Parliament on May 13th 1940" by Winston Churchill

Popularity: 0
Vote
Comment

Posted By C. Tucker Moderator to H- Middle School on 01/16/2012

Read and listen to Winston Churchill's first address to the House of Commons as the Prime Minister (1940). What is the purpose of this speech? What key points does he make about the government, the war and England's objectives as a country? What do you learn about Winston Churchill from this speech?

Once you have posted your response, reply thoughtfully to at least 2 other students. Compliment strong points, ask questions and build on ideas shared!

Timothy13jesus (Poster). "Blood, Toil, Tears and Sweat (given by Winston Churchill)." Online video clip. YouTube. 20 Mar 2009. 12 Oct 2011. http://www.youtube.com/watch?v=gVg7mRheK8>; ;

Attachments

Audio version of Churchill's Speech

Teacher's Note: Winston Churchill's "Blood, Toil, Tears, and Sweat" speech can by copied and pasted directly into the online discussion topic, or a hyperlink can be provided. The speech can be found at www.winstonchurchill.org/learn/speeches/speeches-of-winston-churchill/92-blood-toil-tears-and-sweat.

Common Core Standards

RH.6-8.2, RH.6-8.6, WHST.6-8.4, WHST.6-8.6, WHST.6-8.9

This discussion topic requires that students read Winston Churchill's "Blood, Toil, Tears, and Sweat" speech and listen to an audio recording of Churchill delivering the speech. Students benefit from reading the speech as well as hearing the emotion, points of emphasis, and dramatic pauses in Churchill's delivery.

Once students have read and listened to the speech, they must identify its purpose as well as the central ideas and important points made in the speech. Students are then asked to consider what they learned about Churchill from his speech. To do this they must discuss aspects of the text that reveal his point of view and reflect his character. The integration of media with the audio recording also provides insight into him as a person and his role as a political figure.

Weave Online Work Into the Classroom With Student-Centered Activities

Churchill Museum and Cabinet War Rooms

www.pan3sixty.co.uk/tours/cwr/choose.html

Take a virtual tour of Churchill's War Rooms.

Free

1. *Research.* Put students in groups and have them research Winston Churchill's War Rooms using a computer lab, the library, or home computers. Students create a visual sketch of his War Rooms in groups and should be prepared to present their visuals to the class.

2. *Short Story.* Have students research the Blitz (see suggested resources in the *Teacher's Note* below). Ask them to imagine what a typical day would be like for a Londoner during this bombing campaign. Students then use their research combined with their own imaginations to write a short story detailing a typical day in the life of a Londoner. Encourage students to include sensory details and incorporate actual facts to make their stories more realistic. They should address the following wartime realities in their writing: rationing, curfew, and air raid warnings.

Once students have written their narratives, they can use Pen.io to publish their writing online immediately. They can create their own URL, add photos and videos, and select a theme for their page.

Pen.io

pen.io

Publish writing online quickly. Create a page name, get a personalized URL, select a theme, and add photos and video.

Free

Teacher's Note: History.com has several resources (print and video) about the Blitz.

- "History Features: London Blitz" (video): www.history.com/
videos/history-features-london-blitz#history-features-london-blitz
- "The Blitz Begins" (print): www.history.com/this-day-in-history/
the-blitz-begins
- "British War Cabinet Reacts to the Blitz in Kind" (print): www
.history.com/this-day-in-history/british-war-cabinet-reacts-to
-the-blitz-in-kind

3. *Creative Assignment.* Ask students to imagine they are living in London during the Blitz. They must pack their school backpack with everything they would need to spend 24 hours in a bomb shelter with no notice. They will need to carry these bags around each day, so remind them to choose their items carefully.

This assignment can culminate in a show-and-tell presentation during which students unpack their backpacks in front of the class, explaining why they chose each of the contents included. An alternative is to give students a piece of paper with a tracing of a backpack and ask them to draw what they might carry with them on a daily basis. These could then be hung around the room.

Common Core State Standards: High School History/Social Studies

The following are the literacy standards for history/social studies addressed for high school Grades 9–10 and 11–12 reading standards are listed separately because the language is slightly different. In contrast, the writing standards for all four grades appear together as the language is almost identical.

Grades 9–12 History/Social Studies Literacy Standards Addressed

RH.9-10.1	Cite specific textual evidence to support analysis of primary and secondary sources, attending to such features as the date and origin of the information.	RH.11-12.1	Cite specific textual evidence to support analysis of primary and secondary sources, connecting insights gained from specific details to an understanding of the text as a whole.
RH.9-10.9	Compare and contrast treatments of the same topic in several primary and secondary sources.	RH.11-12.9	Integrate information from diverse sources, both primary and secondary, into a coherent understanding of an idea or event, noting discrepancies among sources.

Grades 9–12 Writing Standards Addressed

WHST.9-12.1	Write arguments focused on *discipline-specific content*.
WHST.9-12.2	Write informative/explanatory texts, including the narration of historical events, scientific procedures/experiments, or technical processes.
WHST.9-12.4	Produce clear and coherent writing in which the development, organization, and style are appropriate to task, purpose, and audience.
WHST.9-12.5	Develop and strengthen writing as needed by planning, revising, editing, rewriting, or trying a new approach, focusing on addressing what is most significant for a specific purpose and audience.
WHST.9-12.6	Use technology, including the Internet, to produce, publish, and update individual or shared writing products in response to ongoing feedback, including new arguments or information.
WHST.9-12.9	Draw evidence from informational texts to support analysis, reflection, and research.

Note: The language describing each standard is taken directly from the Common Core State Standards Initiative website: www.corestandards.org.

As students progress from middle school into high school, they are required to develop their analysis of primary and secondary sources, trace the development of key ideas in a text, understand cause/effect relationships, compare points of view, and evaluate how the structure of a text is used to "advance an explanation or analysis" (Standards RH.9-10.5). In addition to these reading standards, students are also required to continue developing both their informative and argument writing, focusing on discipline-specific content.

Example Online Activity 7.5. George Washington's "Farewell Address" (1796): Analyzing the Forces That Threaten the Nation's Stability

George Washington's "Farewell Address" (1796): Analyzing the Forces That Threatened the Nation's Stability

Posted By C. Tucker Moderator to H- High School on 10/10/2011

Popularity: 0
Vote
Comment

In President Washington's "Farewell Address," he announces his decision not to run for a third term of presidency. In his address he voices concern about the stability of the nation. He identifies 3 specific areas of concern: geographic sectionalism, political factionalism, and interference by foreign powers.

Read his "Farewell Address" and select <u>one</u> of these concerns to discuss in detail:
  • Why does Washington say he is concerned about this?
  • How does it threaten American stability?
  • How does Washington advise the nation to combat this potentially negative force?
  • Do you think his concern was warranted? In the years following his address how did this negative force impact America as a new nation?

Use examples and quotes from Washington's address as well as information learned in this class to support your analysis and explanation.

Once you have posted your response, reply thoughtfully to <u>at least 2</u> other students. Compliment strong points, ask questions and build on ideas shared!

Godliman, Darrel. "USA -- Washington DC -- Washington Monument & Flag." Flag. Flickr. 21 Feb 2009. 10 Nov 2011 Flicker.com [http://www.flickr.com/photos/79986881@N00/3296744537]

Attachments

  ○ geographic sectionalism

  ○ political factionalism

  ○ interference by foreign powers

  ▢ View and Comment (0) ◉ Watch

Common Core Standards

RH.9-12.1, RH.9-12.9, WHST.9-12.2, WHST.9-12.6, WHST.9-12.9

This activity requires students to read President Washington's "Farewell Address," understand the main ideas presented, and analyze the potential threat of forces identified by Washington as potentially dangerous to the United States. To do this effectively they must determine the meaning of complex content-specific vocabulary, such as *factionalism* and *sectionalism*. They must also be able to evaluate the impact of one negative force and how it ultimately affected our nation. Students must demonstrate higher-order thinking and use strong evidence from Washington's address, their textbook, and online research to thoroughly support a clear explanation. This can be the first step toward an informative essay on this topic.

Teacher's Note: George Washington's "Farewell Address" is available at www.access.gpo.gov/congress/senate/farewell/sd106-21.pdf.

Weave Online Work Into the Classroom With Student-Centered Activities

1. *History Comic.* Ask students to select one of the three forces identified by President Washington to focus on for this creative activity. They should design a comic that shows how this threatening force impacted the United States. Students can use thought bubbles to clarify, add detail, or insert humor, but the visuals should be compelling and accurately depict how this force impacted the new nation. This can be done on paper or online using Pixton, an easy-to-use comic maker (for more on Pixton, see p. 105).

2. *Discussion.* Start this conversation in small groups, then discuss as a class. Ask each group to discuss the following questions:

My Fake Wall

myfakewall.com

Create fake Facebook-style profiles for historical figures or literary characters.

Beta version

Free

- What do you learn about George Washington's character from his decision to step down after two terms as president?
- Why was this an important precedent to set?
- What attributes, qualities, or characteristics do you believe Washington possessed?
- Why has Washington been called the greatest man to ever live?

Create a My Fake Wall or Facebook page for George Washington that reveals aspects of his personality and character while providing insights into his relationships, interest, hopes, and fears.

3. *Group Activity.* Divide the class into groups, and give each group 1 of the 10 original amendments to the U.S. Constitution. Each group should discuss how their amendment would specifically combat a potential threat to the nation identified by Washington in his "Farewell Address." Each

> **Study Blue**
>
> *www.studyblue.com*
>
> Students create online flashcards, quizzes, and study guides to share.
>
> Free

group can create a poster for their amendment to hang on the wall as a visual reminder of what that amendment said and what it was intended to accomplish. These poster projects could also be done online using a tool like Glogster (for more on Glogster, see p. 93) to make the visuals interactive with multimedia.

Students can also use Study Blue to create online flashcards for each amendment as well as for other important historical people, places, events, and terms.

Example Online Activity 7.6. Franklin D. Roosevelt's "State of the Union Address": Should the United States Have Entered World War II?

Teacher's Note: The transcript of Franklin D. Roosevelt's "State of the Union Address" is available at www.americanrhetoric.com/speeches/fdrthefourfreedoms.htm.

Common Core Standards

RH.9-12.1, WHST.9-12.1, WHST.9-12.4, WHST.9-12.5, WHST.9-12.6, WHST.9-12.9

Students read and listen to President Roosevelt's "State of the Union Address" to evaluate his reasons for supporting the United States' entry into World War II. Students need to evaluate both the costs and benefits of going to war as stated in President Roosevelt's speech. Then they should compare that to the information they have learned from their text and online research.

Students must form a clear opinion stating that they either agree or disagree with President Roosevelt's decision to enter World War II.

Franklin D. Roosevelt's "State of the Union Address:" Should the United States Have Entered World War II?

Popularity: 0
Vote
Comment

Posted By C. Tucker Moderator to H- High School on 10/05/2011

- -

Listen to President Roosevelt's "State of the Union Address." Think about the costs versus the benefits of entering World War II as stated in this speech. Do you think the United States should have entered the war? Why or why not?

Vote yes or no and clearly state your position. Focus on <u>3 reasons</u> why you believe the United States should or should not have entered World War II. Use details and quotes from this speech as well as online research to support your claims.

Once you have written and posted your rough draft argument essay, read the writing posted by <u>at least 3</u> of your peers and provide them with detailed feedback on their writing.

ClassicNewsClips (Poster). "Franklin D. Roosevelt 'Four Freedoms' Speech- January 6, 1941." Online video clip." YouTube. 25 Feb 2011. 12 Oct 2011 http://www.youtube.com/watch?v=QnrZUHcpoNA style="font-style: italic;">

Attachments

Excerpt from Franklin D. Roosevelt's

Then they need to provide three clear reasons for their position and support those reasons with concrete details from multiple sources. These three reasons will each be developed into a body paragraph for the final argument paper.

In the discussion phase of this activity, students need to evaluate the strength and credibility of their peers' claims and consider counterarguments to be addressed in their own essays. It is significantly easier for students to address counterarguments in their writing when they have had an opportunity to discuss them online with their peers first. This dialogue is invaluable to raising students' awareness of other perspectives and arguments.

Weave Online Work Into the Classroom With Student-Centered Activities

1. *Comparing Primary and Secondary Sources.* Provide students with a primary and secondary account of the attack on Pearl Harbor. Then ask them to consider the following questions:

- How do they each discuss the same moment in history?
- Compare the two points of view. What are the similarities and differences in each account?
- What is the significance of those similarities and differences?

Start this conversation in small groups, then discuss as a class.

Teacher's Note: History.com provides a strong secondary source on this topic: www.history.com/topics/pearl-harbor.

2. *Creative Project.* Ask students, in small groups, to create a visual timeline of events from the start of World War II to the United States' decision to enter the war. This visual timeline should pair important dates and events with visual representations of those events. This can be done online using Tiki-Toki (for more on Tiki-Toki, see p. 102) to create an interactive multimedia timeline with text, video, and images.

3. *Research.* In small groups, students research how propaganda was used to rally support for the United States' involvement in the war. Students should select specific examples of propaganda to analyze as a group.

- Who is being stereotyped in these images?
- What messages do these propaganda posters attempt to send the American people?
- What fears are exploited in this propaganda?

As groups, students share their findings with the class and discuss common themes present in World War II propaganda.

Then students can work in groups to create their own example of propaganda that reflects a form of pressure or social messaging they

PicMonkey

www.picmonkey.com

Photo editing with possible collage feature coming soon.

Free

feel from society, media, parents, and/or friends. This will help them better understand propaganda—the purpose, messaging, and effect. Students can make their examples of present-day propaganda by hand, or they can use a photo-editing tool like PicMonkey to upload and edit images and include text.

Teacher's Note: Life.com has a variety of examples of World War II propaganda.

Chapter Summary

The history standards are integrated into the English reading and writing standards for K–5 because these subjects are often taught together in elementary grades. The standards emphasize the importance of reading to build a strong understanding of history. As a result, I used the "Informational Text: Literary Nonfiction and Historical, Scientific, and Technical Texts" list provided by the Common Core State Standards to design questions that address the reading and writing standards for English in Grades K–5 but are focused on historical texts. These questions combine reading and writing, which is easier to accomplish when teachers can embed supplementary historical documents online to drive online discussions and writing assignments.

In Grades 6–12 the writing standards for history emphasize argument and informative writing, but the Standards also state that narrative elements and techniques should be woven into these types of writing to make them more engaging. If online discussions and writing assignments are a consistent part of the curriculum, then students will improve their writing skills through practice. Many of the writing prompts in this chapter can be developed into process papers if teachers want to build on the work done online.

Using online discussions, debates, and group work requires that students think critically about historical texts—speeches, articles, primary and secondary sources—to support their opinions, arguments, and statements. Many of these questions and follow-up student-centered activities require research online to supplement the information presented in class. This provides opportunities for students to think critically about media, identify bias, and evaluate different points of view.

This chapter provides examples of how media can be used to make history more real and relevant for students. If they can see photographs, documentary clips, and newspaper articles, then moments from history come to life for them. As a result, I have embedded media in all of my activities to highlight how effective a learning platform or learning management system can be when introducing historical events.

Book Study Questions

1. How do you currently support the development of reading and writing in your history/social studies curriculum? What do students typically read? What do they do when they read— take notes, annotate, discuss? How might you use online discussions to engage them in conversations about reading?

2. Is it a challenge to find primary and secondary documents to use with students? If so, how do you deal with this challenge? How would using an online space to embed digital copies of sources make it easier to share a variety of primary and secondary sources with students? If you currently use primary and secondary sources, where do you find them and how do you make them available to students?

3. How often do you engage students in debates about historical or social studies topics? Would using the yes/no question type make this easier for you to do? What impact would engaging students in an online debate have on their understanding of a topic? How could a follow-up debate in class complement the online work?

4. How do you currently use media in your curriculum? What types do you use? What is the biggest hurdle you face in using media? How do your students respond to media? Where do you find it? Do you have resources you would recommend for quality media for history and social studies teachers?

5. How can media help you support lower-level readers in your class to better understand primary and secondary sources? What kinds of media could you use to make reading historical documents more accessible and less intimidating? What are the benefits of having students listen to a recording or watch a clip from a speech or documentary in addition to reading a text?

6. How do you currently incorporate writing into your history/ social studies curriculum? What challenges do you face teaching writing? How might you address these challenges using a blended instruction approach to writing? How would you engage students in a peer editing process online? How would the online space help you improve your writing program? Brainstorm creative approaches to writing using a blended learning model.

7. How can using an online learning platform help you scaffold writing assignments in a way that better supports all students to ensure they reach grade-level proficiency in writing? Think about a writing assignment you currently use with students— how could you use the online space to better support students during the different parts of the writing process?

8. How might you use online media tools to allow students to explore digital writing and multimedia projects to develop media literacy? Would you like to have students create documentaries using iMovie or create propaganda posters using Glogster or PicMonkey? How would assigning multimedia projects inspire students to think more deeply about their work and the subject?

8

Science

There is a national focus on science, technology, engineering, and math (STEM) due to a dramatic decrease in students pursuing degrees in STEM subjects into and beyond secondary school. The challenge is to get students interested in science at a young age and maintain that interest through secondary school. Students need to see the connection between the topics they study in science and their lives beyond the classroom.

Technology integration has the potential to increase student interest with hands-on activities, labs, experiments, fieldwork, model building, and research-based problem solving. Actively engaging students in the science curriculum makes complex ideas more concrete and intelligible. Students must understand the relevance of science to their own lives; technology can create this bridge.

Common Core State Standards: Upper Elementary Science

The following are the reading informational text standards addressed for the upper elementary grades. I have used the English language arts Grades 4–5 reading informational text standards and writing standards because the science standards are integrated into the English standards until sixth grade. The Grades 4–5 writing standards appear together as the language is almost identical.

Grades 4–5 Reading Information Standards Addressed

RI.4.1	Refer to details and examples in a text when explaining what the text says explicitly and when drawing inferences from the text.	RI.5.1	Quote accurately from a text when explaining what the text says explicitly and when drawing inferences from the text.
RI.4.2	Determine the main idea of a text and explain how it is supported by key details; summarize the text.	RI.5.4	Determine the meaning of general academic and domain-specific words and phrases in a text relevant to a *Grade 5 topic or subject area.*
RI.4.4	Determine the meaning of general academic and domain-specific words or phrases in a text relevant to a *Grade 4 topic or subject area.*	RI.5.7	Draw on information from multiple print or digital sources, demonstrating the ability to locate an answer to a question quickly or to solve a problem efficiently.

Grades 4–5 Writing Standards Addressed

W.4-5.1	Write opinion pieces on topics or texts, supporting a point of view with reasons and information.
W.4-5.2	Write informative/explanatory texts to examine a topic and convey ideas and information clearly.
W.4-5.4	Produce clear and coherent writing in which the development and organization are appropriate to task, purpose, and audience.
W.4-5.6	With some guidance and support from adults, use technology, including the Internet, to produce and publish writing as well as to interact and collaborate with others.
W.4-5.7	Conduct short research projects that use several sources to build knowledge through investigation of different aspects of a topic.
W.4-5.9	Draw evidence from literary or informational texts to support analysis, reflection, and research.

Note: The language describing each standard is taken directly from the Common Core State Standards Initiative website: www.corestandards.org.

Because elementary teachers teach all subjects in a single day, they tend to integrate the various subjects. As a result, the standards for science in the elementary grades, similar to those in history, are incorporated into the K–5 English language arts reading and writing standards. I used the list of "Texts Illustrating the Complexity, Quality, and Range for Student Reading K–5" in the Common Core State Standards for Grades 4–5 on science topics to design these upper elementary topics. They require students to demonstrate fluency in reading and writing while focusing on science topics and content. The student-centered in-class activities that follow each example online discussion question are focused on tasks that can be extended with a technology component. These activities create opportunities for students to research, explore, and discuss topics of interest.

Incorporating an online component into a traditional science class also addresses the Common Core State Standards' need to integrate technology. Simultaneously, it creates more time and space to engage students in meaningful conversations to help them better understand the curriculum that seems to be alienating so many young people.

Example Online Activity 8.1. After Reading *Discovering Mars: The Amazing Story of the Red Planet,* Do You Think the Government Should Spend Money to Explore Mars?

Common Core Standards

RI.4.1, RI.4-5.4, RI.5.7, W.4-5.1, W.4-5.4, W.4-5.6, W.4-5.9

This question assumes students have read *Discovering Mars: The Amazing Story of the Red Planet.* (*Note:* Another text or article about Mars can be used instead.) They must think critically about the benefits of exploring Mars, then weigh those benefits against the financial costs of space exploration. Students must form a clear opinion about whether they think the government should fund the exploration of Mars and support their position with a clear explanation and examples. This question requires students to understand and think deeply about their reading, while using examples from a text and online research to support opinion writing.

This question also combines two high-interest topics for many kids—space and money. Most kids are fascinated by space, the potential of finding life on other planets, and the possibility of humans inhabiting other planets. This encourages them to think about the benefits of the U.S. space program, which has recently undergone severe financial cuts. It also ties this topic to the very real issue of money and how money is spent in this country. In these tough economic times, many kids are being personally affected by money and the power it holds. Tapping into their awareness of the state of the economy allows them to bridge the gap between space exploration and their own lives. This creates a real-world connection that can be valuable in engaging and maintaining interest.

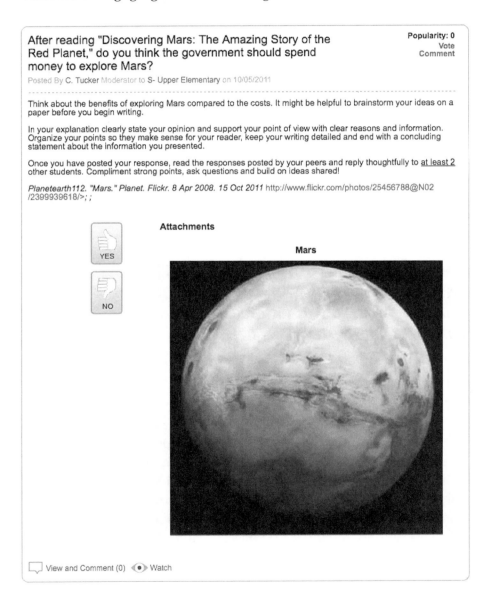

Weave Online Work Into the Classroom With Student-Centered Activities

1. *Follow-Up Debate.* Project or recreate the results of the online debate on the board, then facilitate a follow-up discussion in the classroom.

Revisit main points made in the online conversation, address unanswered questions, and ask students if their perspectives changed as a result of their online debate. If students voted against funding the exploration of Mars, ask them where they think the government should be spending money. Students can brainstorm where they think the government should spend money using an online canvas like Lino (for more on Lino, see p. 126).

2. *Sensory Walk.* In small groups have students imagine what Mars would be like in terms of their senses. Ask them to brainstorm their ideas on paper or online using a virtual bulletin board like Corkboard.

- See?
- Hear?
- Smell?
- Taste?
- Touch or feel?

This will require that they use their imaginations as well as details from their reading.

Corkboard.me

corkboard.me

Instantly create a virtual corkboard where students can brainstorm ideas with colorful sticky notes. Students working on the corkboard can engage in live chat as they work to collaborate more effectively.

Free	Pro
Instantly launch a public corkboard with a unique URL	Up to 5 corkboards with custom settings Password-protected with private access controls Secure 256-bit SSL encrypted data transfer Custom URLs Priority 24/7 email support
Free	$4.99 per month

---

3. *Found Poetry.* Ask students to read an article about Mars or a short story from Ray Bradbury's *The Martian Chronicles*. In groups students should discuss how Mars is portrayed in the reading—was it similar

to or different from what they expected? Ask students to write a found poem about Mars using key lines, phrases, and words from the supplementary reading provided. Students can publish their poems online using Pen.io (for more on Pen.io, see p. 128).

Example Online Activity 8.2.
What Causes Hurricanes?

What causes hurricanes?

Posted By C. Tucker Moderator to S- Upper Elementary on 10/05/2011

Popularity: 0
Vote
Comment

Clearly describe the cause of hurricanes using details and facts from Patricia Lauber's book "Hurricanes: Earth's Mightiest Storms" to support your explanation. Remember to develop your discussion of hurricanes with examples and end your explanation with a concluding statement about the importance of this topic.

Once you have posted your response, reply thoughtfully to at least 2 other students. Compliment strong points, ask questions, suggest facts that would improve their explanation and build on ideas shared!

NASA Goddard Photo and Video. "Hurricane Katrina." Hurricane. Flickr. 28 Aug 2005. 17 Oct 2011.
http://www.flickr.com/photos/24662369@N07/4923521946/
style="mso-bidi-font-style:normal">

Attachments
Hurricane Katrina Satellite Image

Common Core Standards

RI.4-5.1, W.4-5.1, W.4-5.4, W.4-5.6, W.4-5.9

Given the lack of stability and the volatility associated with extreme weather, this is a subject that many students find interesting. Hurricanes, in particular, have stormed onto the national stage with the devastation of Hurricane Katrina, which hit New Orleans in 2005. A conversation about hurricanes can be linked to a discussion about the effects of climate change and how it is causing a dramatic increase in the frequency and intensity of hurricanes around the world.

This writing task asks students to read a text on hurricanes and explain in their own words what causes them. To do this effectively, they must understand key vocabulary and be able to discuss the different factors that work together to create a hurricane. Finally, students must be able to introduce their topic clearly and support their explanation of what causes hurricanes with specific facts and details from the reading.

Weave Online Work Into the Classroom With Student-Centered Activities

1. *Read and Discuss.* Provide students with a news article and an eyewitness account of Hurricane Katrina—one of the most devastating hurricanes to hit the United States. Ask students to compare these accounts to the descriptions of hurricanes they have read about in their text. In groups, have them discuss the following questions:

> **HurricaneKatrina.com**
>
> *hurricanekatrina.com*
>
> Nonprofit site with articles, pictures, personal stories, and links related to Hurricane Katrina.
>
> Free

- How are the accounts similar to or different from one another?
- Did the article, eyewitness account, or text have the biggest impact on you?
- Why do you think this particular source made such an impact on you?
- What did you learn about Hurricane Katrina and hurricanes in general?
- How many people, animals, and homes were affected?
- What was your emotional response to seeing the photographs?

This can be extended into an artistic project asking students to create a multimedia presentation using Glogster (for more on Glogster, see p. 93).

Weebly

education.weebly.com

Create a website with a blog using the easy drag-and-drop Web builder. Includes multimedia features, stable cloud hosting, and hundreds of available themes.

Free	Pro
1 site with unlimited pages	10 sites per account with unlimited pages per student website
5 MB limit per file uploaded	100 MB file uploads
Includes images and text	Audio and video player
	Embedded documents
	Password-protect individual pages
	Premium support
	Remove or customize Weebly footer
	$39.95 per year

2. *Research and Chart.* In small groups, have students research the frequency and strength of hurricanes in the last 10 years using credible online resources to better understand extreme weather trends. Once they have completed the research, allow them to discuss the following questions as a group:

- What did you learn about the frequency of hurricanes?
- Where are they occurring?
- How do you evaluate the strength of these hurricanes?
- Can your group identify any patterns? What might be causing these trends?

UNISYS

weather.unisys.com/hurricane/atlantic

Track tropical storms in the Atlantic Ocean by year. View storm patterns and intensity.

Free

Students can create a poster of their findings or work together to design an informational Weebly website to present information about hurricanes, trends, climate change, and more.

Give each group a blank world map, and ask them to

chart their findings using color-coded labels. The UNISYS website has a list of hurricanes that have hit the Atlantic Ocean since 1851. Students can select a year and view a map of the Atlantic with each hurricane mapped to show its trajectory and color-coded to reflect its strength. The maps are followed by a chart detailing date, wind speed, and pressure. This resource makes it possible for students to view a series of years and chart the hurricanes on a master map, which can be used to discuss trends and address the questions above.

3. *Group Investigation.* Divide the class into small groups, and give each group a natural disaster to research—earthquakes, tornados, tsunamis, volcanic eruptions, avalanches, or blizzards. Have students work together in their groups to answer the following questions using online research or textbooks and/or supplementary reading supplied by the teacher:

- What regions experience this type of natural disaster?
- What are the scientific causes of this natural disaster?
- What did you learn about the frequency and strength of this natural disaster?
- How does this type of natural disaster impact humans?

Students can create an informational poster about their natural disaster to present and display in the classroom. To extend this assignment online, students could use their research to create an informational website about their natural disaster using Wix (for more on Wix, see p. 101) or Weebly (see p. 146).

> ### National Geographic
>
> *environment.nationalgeographic.com/ environment/natural-disasters*
>
> Find information on a variety of natural disasters. Select a natural disaster, view photos, and read detailed information on that natural disaster.
>
> Free

Teacher's Note: National Geographic is an excellent resource for information on natural disasters.

Common Core State Standards: Middle School Science

The following are the literacy standards for science addressed for middle school. The literacy and writing standards for Grades 6–8 are combined in the standards just as they appear below.

Grades 6–8 Literacy in Science Standards Addressed

RST.6-8.1	Cite specific textual evidence to support analysis of science and technical texts.
RST.6-8.4	Determine the meaning of symbols, key terms, and other domain-specific words and phrases as they are used in a specific scientific or technical context relevant to *Grades 6–8 texts and topics.*
RST.6-8.7	Integrate quantitative or technical information expressed in words in a text with a version of that information expressed visually (e.g., in a flowchart, diagram, model, graph, or table).

Grades 6–8 Writing Standards Addressed

WHST.6-8.2	Write informative/explanatory texts, including the narration of historical events, scientific procedures/experiments, or technical processes.
WHST.6-8.4	Produce clear and coherent writing in which the development, organization, and style are appropriate to task, purpose, and audience.
WHST.6-8.6	Use technology, including the Internet, to produce and publish writing and present the relationships between information and ideas clearly and efficiently.
WHST.6-8.9	Draw evidence from informational texts to support analysis, reflection, and research.

Note: The language describing each standard is taken directly from the Common Core State Standards Initiative website: www.corestandards.org.

In Grades 6–8 the reading standards for science are separated from the English language arts standards. Students in middle school should be able to identify and discuss textual evidence, summarize information, understand key scientific vocabulary, recognize the author's purpose, and compare information displayed in different forms. They also need to "distinguish among fact, opinion, and reasoned judgment based on research" (Standards RH.6-8.8) and "compare and contrast the information gained from experiments, simulations, video, or multimedia sources with that gained from reading a text on the same topic" (Standards RST.6-8.9). The following questions and student-centered extension activities give students opportunities to develop these skills. In addition, argument and informative writing must also be taught in science in Grades 6–12.

Example Online Activity 8.3. Energy Flow in an Ecosystem: Producers, Consumers, and Decomposers

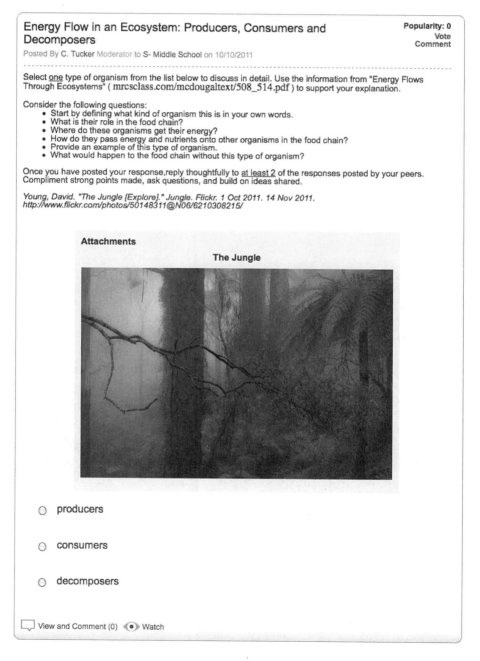

Energy Flow in an Ecosystem: Producers, Consumers and Decomposers   Popularity: 0
                                                                                          Vote
Posted By C. Tucker Moderator to S- Middle School on 10/10/2011   Comment

- -

Select <u>one</u> type of organism from the list below to discuss in detail. Use the information from "Energy Flows Through Ecosystems" (mrcsclass.com/mcdougaltext/508_514.pdf) to support your explanation.

Consider the following questions:
- Start by defining what kind of organism this is in your own words.
- What is their role in the food chain?
- Where do these organisms get their energy?
- How do they pass energy and nutrients onto other organisms in the food chain?
- Provide an example of this type of organism.
- What would happen to the food chain without this type of organism?

Once you have posted your response, reply thoughtfully to <u>at least 2</u> of the responses posted by your peers. Compliment strong points made, ask questions, and build on ideas shared.

Young, David. "The Jungle [Explore]." Jungle. Flickr. 1 Oct 2011. 14 Nov 2011.
http://www.flickr.com/photos/50148311@N06/6210308215/

Attachments

The Jungle

○   producers

○   consumers

○   decomposers

▢ View and Comment (0)   ◉ Watch

Common Core Standards

RST.6-8.1, RST.6-8.4, RST.6-8.7, WHST.6-8.2, WHST.6-8.4, WHST.6-8.6, WHST.6-8.9

Once students have read the document, they must explain and analyze the information to accurately describe the energy flow in an ecosystem. Students only focus on one type of organism in an ecosystem, but they benefit from the explanations of their peers. It can be easier to understand complex concepts when they are explained and discussed with classmates. Students can ask questions and make connections between the various types of organisms in a given ecosystem. Students do not have to understand every aspect of a topic to participate in an online conversation, and they learn a great deal from interacting with their peers, as each student contributes a part of the overall picture.

Teacher's Note: This online discussion question requires that students read "Energy Flows Through Ecosystems" and demonstrate an understanding of different types of organisms in an ecosystem. This document can be found at http://tinyurl.com/7kx7wd7.

Weave Online Work Into the Classroom With Student-Centered Activities

Virtual Teacher Aid

www.vtaide.com/png/foodwebFF.htm

Design a food web using images and arrows.

Free

1. *Group Investigation.* Divide the class into small groups, and give each group an ecosystem to explore. Ask students to work together to draw the food cycle they would expect to find in that ecosystem. They will need to identify specific producers, consumers, and decomposers for their particular ecosystem. Students will include pictures (drawn or cut out from a magazine) of plants, animals, and insects and need to show the flow of energy and nutrients with arrows (remind them that it will look more like a web than a circle). Students can create an online food web using the food web creator on the Virtual Teacher Aid site.

2. *Research and Think Critically.* Divide the class into small groups, and have them research the 2010 BP oil spill. Ask students to discuss the impacts of this disaster on the ecosystem in the Gulf of Mexico, specifically the impact on producers, consumers, and decomposers. Then

each group should visually show the way the ecosystem and food chain has been disrupted as a result of this oil spill. This can be done on poster paper or online using Lino (for more on Lino, see p. 126) to combine photos, video, and text.

Teacher's Note: The White House website is a good starting point for credible information on the BP oil spill: www.whitehouse.gov/deepwater-bp-oil-spill. The Environmental Protection Agency is another resource for news released to this topic: www.epa.gov/bpspill. Remind students that there may be bias involved depend-

> **Mongabay**
>
> *rainforests.mongabay.com/amazon/rainforest_ecology.html*
>
> Explore information on rainforests—geography, climate, precipitation, canopy structure, independence of organisms, and links.
>
> Free

ing on the news source—even the White House. Discuss strategies for identifying and dealing with bias.

3. *Read and Analyze.* Provide students with an article or other resource that discusses the destruction of rainforests around the globe. Give them time to read the article individually or in groups, then ask them to discuss the following questions (first in small groups, then as a class):

- Why are rainforests such an important ecosystem?
- What are the global effects of cutting down rainforests?
- Why are rainforests being cut down?
- How does this impact climate change?

Example Online Activity 8.4.
Density and Buoyancy: Sink or Float?

Common Core Standards

RST.6-8.1, RST.6-8.4, WHST.6-8.2, WHST.6-8.6, WHST.6-8.9

Students begin by making predictions about whether they think specific objects will sink or float based on their understanding of density and buoyancy. To do this, they must understand the relationship between these concepts. They have to form a clear hypothesis and support their informed guesses with evidence gathered during research. There may also be unknown variables they have to consider in answering the question. Students will reach different conclusions,

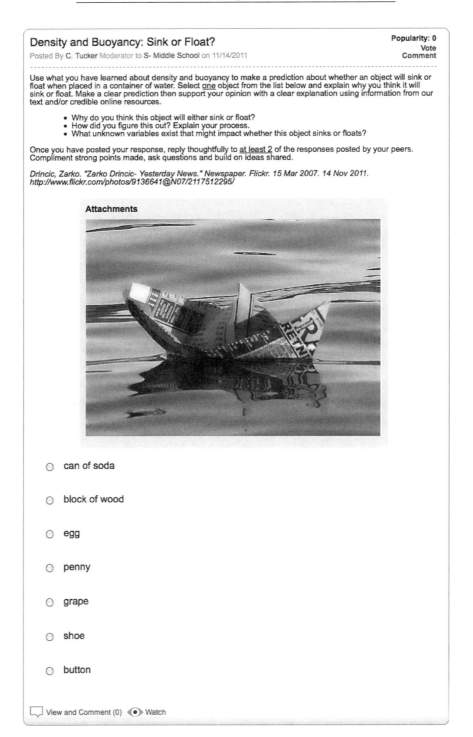

Density and Buoyancy: Sink or Float?

Posted By C. Tucker Moderator to S- Middle School on 11/14/2011

Popularity: 0
Vote
Comment

Use what you have learned about density and buoyancy to make a prediction about whether an object will sink or float when placed in a container of water. Select <u>one</u> object from the list below and explain why you think it will sink or float. Make a clear prediction then support your opinion with a clear explanation using information from our text and/or credible online resources.

- Why do you think this object will either sink or float?
- How did you figure this out? Explain your process.
- What unknown variables exist that might impact whether this object sinks or floats?

Once you have posted your response, reply thoughtfully to <u>at least 2</u> of the responses posted by your peers. Compliment strong points made, ask questions and build on ideas shared.

Drincic, Zarko. "Zarko Drincic- Yesterday News." Newspaper. Flickr. 15 Mar 2007. 14 Nov 2011.
http://www.flickr.com/photos/9136641@N07/2117512295/

Attachments

○ can of soda

○ block of wood

○ egg

○ penny

○ grape

○ shoe

○ button

View and Comment (0) ◉ Watch

and the online discussion component provides a space to question each other's predictions, ask questions, and learn from the explanations of their peers.

Weave Online Work Into the Classroom With Student-Centered Activities

1. *Labs.* Divide the class into lab groups, and give each group a collection of objects from the list presented online. Ask them to conduct their own experiments, testing each hypothesis and recording the results. These results should then be used as a starting place for a discussion about whether their results were in line with their predictions. What object was most surprising? If class time is limited, online lab groups can be created to give students the time and space to discuss the results of their experiments online.

2. *Research and Think Critically.* Ask students to research the sinking of the Titanic, which was often referred to as an "unsinkable" ship. How did it lose its buoyancy? What caused the Titanic to sink? Relate this to density and buoyancy. This can be extended into a creative project by asking students to create a series of drawings or sketches showing how they think the Titanic sank. Each picture should include an explanation of what is happening in relation to density, buoyancy, and the other variables present.

Teacher's Note: History.com has a video titled "The Titanic's Structure," featuring naval architect Roger Long, that discusses the structure of the boat: www.history.com/videos/titanic-roger-long---naval-architect.

3. *Labs.* Divide the class into lab groups, and ask them to test the buoyancy of objects in salt water versus fresh water. Before conducting their experiment, they must consider predictions about how the salt content in the water impacts an object's ability to float. Each group should form a hypothesis supported by evidence, test a variety of objects in the different types of water, and record results and discuss: Why do some objects float in one but sink in the other?

Common Core State Standards: High School Science

The following are the literacy standards for history/social studies addressed for high school. The Grades 9–12 writing standards appear together as the language is almost identical.

Grades 9–10 and 11–12 Science Literacy Standards Addressed

RST.9-10.4	Determine the meaning of symbols, key terms, and other domain-specific words and phrases as they are used in a specific scientific or technical context relevant to *Grades 9–10 texts and topics*.
RST.11-12.4	Determine the meaning of symbols, key terms, and other domain-specific words and phrases as they are used in a specific scientific or technical context relevant to *Grades 11–12 texts and topics*.
RST.11-12.7	Integrate and evaluate multiple sources of information presented in diverse formats and media (e.g., quantitative data, video, multimedia) in order to address a question or solve a problem.
RST.11-12.8	Evaluate the hypotheses, data, analysis, and conclusions in a science or technical text, verifying the data when possible and corroborating or challenging conclusions with other sources of information.
RST.11-12.9	Synthesize information from a range of sources (e.g., texts, experiments, simulations) into a coherent understanding of a process, phenomenon, or concept, resolving conflicting information when possible.

Grades 9–12 Writing Standards Addressed

WHST.9-12.1	Write arguments focused on *discipline-specific content*.
WHST.9-12.2	Write informative/explanatory texts, including the narration of historical events, scientific procedures/ experiments, or technical processes.
WHST.9-12.4	Produce clear and coherent writing in which the development, organization, and style are appropriate to task, purpose, and audience.
WHST.9-12.6	Use technology, including the Internet, to produce, publish, and update individual or shared writing products in response to ongoing feedback, including new arguments or information.
WHST.9-12.9	Draw evidence from informational texts to support analysis, reflection, and research.

Note: The language describing each standard is taken directly from the Common Core State Standards Initiative website: www.corestandards.org.

Example Online Activity 8.5. A. Cell Biology: Prokaryotic Cell or Eukaryotic Cell?

Cell Biology: Prokaryotic Cell or Eukaryotic Cell?

Posted By C. Tucker Moderator to S- High School on 10/10/2011

Popularity: 0
Vote
Comment

What type of cell is this: prokaryotic or eukaryotic?

Select your answer then justify your decision by explaining the parts of the cell structure that helped you to label it. When referencing specific cell structures, explain what they are and what they do in your own words. Use the textbook and/or credible online resources to help you correctly identify this cell. Conclude by explaining the primary purpose of this type of cell and identify any parts of the cell you found difficult to label.

Once you have posted your response, reply thoughtfully to at least 3 of your classmates. Compliment strong points made, ask questions, answer any questions posed, and build on ideas presented.

[Note: Remove citation prior to posting!]
The Science Floor (Briercliffe, Tre). "Eukaryotic Cell." Cell. Flickr. 1 Dec 2008. 14 Nov 2011. http://www.flickr.com/photos/23473127@N02/3081734787/

Attachments

???

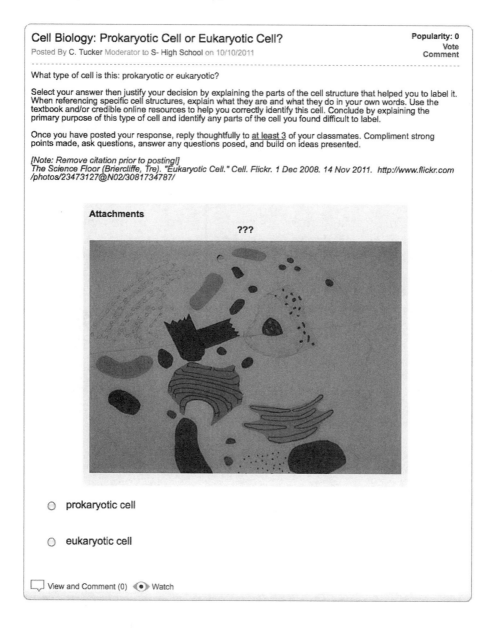

○   prokaryotic cell

○   eukaryotic cell

⬚ View and Comment (0)   ◉ Watch

Common Core Standards

RST.9-12.4, WHST.9-12.2, WHST.9-12.4, WHST.9-12.6, WHST.9-12.9

Students must apply their knowledge of cell structure to identify this cell based on the features present. They must support their answer with a clear explanation and evidence.

Weave Online Work Into the Classroom With Student-Centered Activities

Biology Junction

www.biologyjunction.com/biology_coloring_worksheets.htm

Download printable biology worksheets, including cell structure sheets.

Free

1. *Creative Assignment.* Divide the class into small groups, then give each an unlabeled plant cell and an unlabeled animal cell. (See sidebar about Biology Junction.) Ask students to work together to identify the type of cell, color the cell structures, and label the different parts of each cell.

2. *Artistic Project.* Have students work in pairs to build a model of a plant or animal cell. Encourage them to be as creative as they like with the materials they use. Each group then presents its model, explains why certain materials were used, and identifies the parts of the cell.

An alternative is to have students use an online drawing tool like Queeky to draw different types of cells to print, label, and share.

Queeky

www.queeky.com/app

Create a free online drawing that can be printed, shared, or saved.

Free

Lucid Chart

www.lucidchart.com

Create online Venn diagrams, flow charts, and diagrams.

Free

3. *Compare/Contrast Activity.* Ask students to work in groups to identify the similarities and differences between a prokaryotic cell and a eukaryotic cell. They should use the information they brainstormed to fill in a Venn diagram on paper or online using Lucid Chart. Groups should be prepared to share their Venn diagrams with the class.

Example Online Activity 8.6. Debate:
Do You Think Cloning Should Be Banned?

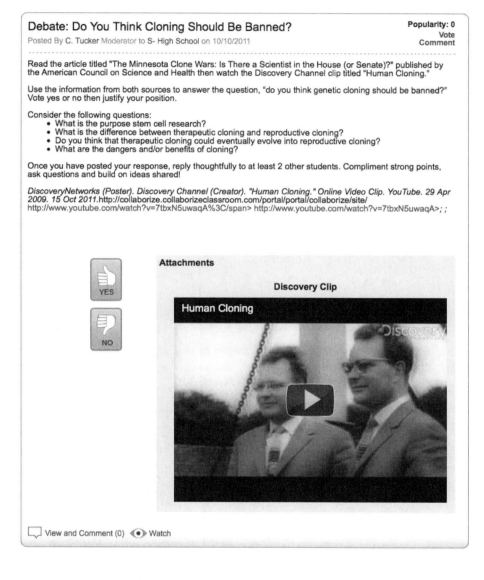

Cloning is an interesting and highly debated topic. This question asks students to read the article "The (Minnesota) Clone Wars: Is There a Scientist in the House (or Senate)?" published by the American Council on Science and Health.

Teacher's Note: This article is available at www.acsh.org/factsfears/ newsid.2493/news_detail.asp. Another good resource is The Discovery Channel's documentary clip "Human Cloning," which can be found at youtube/7tbxN5uwaqA.

Common Core Standards

RST.11-12.7, RST.11-12.8, RST.11-12.9, WHST.9-12.1, WHST.9-12.4, WHST.9-12.6, WHST.9-12.9

Students need to consider the views and possible biases present in each form of media. They must weigh the benefits of cloning against the dangers and potential problems to form a clear argument either for or against cloning. The discussion component of this question exposes them to the perspectives of their peers, forcing them to consider counterarguments.

Weave Online Work Into the Classroom With Student-Centered Activities

1. *Follow-Up Debate*

ProConLists.com

www.proconlists.com

Create a pro versus con list about any question or topic to help weigh the positives and negatives on an issue.

Free

- Take the results of the online discussion, and display them on the board. Then have a follow-up debate about whether cloning should be banned.
- Ask students to reflect on the online discussion. Did it impact their point of view?
- Have students argue the opposing point of view so they thoroughly consider the counterarguments.
- Create a pro versus con list on paper or online using ProConLists .com.

2. *Read and Think Critically.* Ask students to read about Dolly—the domestic sheep that was cloned in 1996—and discuss what they learned about her life and death.

- How was Dolly cloned?
- How was Dolly similar to or different from other sheep?
- What health problems did she experience that resulted from being cloned?

- What did scientists learn about cloning from her life and death?
- Has this research impacted your opinion about cloning?

Teacher's Note: The Human Genome Project Information website provides information on cloning, animals being cloned (including Dolly), and the risks of cloning: www.ornl.gov/sci/techresources/Human_ Genome/elsi/cloning.shtml. AnimalResearch.info also has information on Dolly: www.animalresearch.info/en/listing/151/cloning -dolly-the-sheep/.

3. *Research.* Investigate stem cell research. How are stem cells used? What is the controversy surrounding stem cell research? Once students have researched stem cells and how they relate to cloning, ask students to create an informational poster about the uses of stem cells and the debate around stem cell research or an online poster or brochure using Glogster (for more on Glogster, see p. 93).

Teacher's Note: The National Institutes of Health provides information on stem cells ranging from a basic overview to ethical issues: stemcells.nih.gov/info/basics.

Chapter Summary

Like history, the science standards for K–5 are integrated into the English reading and writing standards. I have used the "Informational Text: Literary Nonfiction and Historical, Scientific, and Technical Texts" list provided by the Common Core State Standards to design questions that address the reading and writing standards for English in Grades 4–5 but are focused on science topics. My goal was to design upper elementary discussion questions and tasks that focus on high-interest topics because the biggest challenge in science is maintaining interest into secondary school. Each online discussion topic requires students to complete a reading on a subject related to science—Mars or Hurricanes—then complete a writing task related to that topic.

The online discussion topics and activities for middle school and high school require students to do both reading and research. They must learn how to find credible research online as well as analyze and synthesize that information. In addition to the online work, the student-centered activities are focused on creative tasks and labs. Students are encouraged to share what they have learned via creative posters, online collages, or informational websites.

The writing standards focus on argument and informative writing in science, so I designed questions that require students to practice those types of writings. If online discussions and writing assignments are a consistent part of the curriculum, then students will improve their writing skills through practice.

In addition to supporting teachers in developing their writing program in science, online discussions create opportunities for students to access a support network of their peers who can answer questions and clarify confusion. If students have a space to discuss complex science topics, they are more likely to stay engaged in the curriculum.

In this chapter I focused on designing example discussion topics that address both reading and writing standards, while effectively integrating a technology component to allow students to publish writing, collaborate with peers, and complete research projects.

Book Study Questions

1. How do you make science relevant for students? What connections do you make between science and real-life situations that students are curious about? Is it a challenge to connect the science curriculum to their lives? How can the integration of technology into your science curriculum increase student interest?

2. How do you currently support the development of reading and writing in your science curriculum? What do students typically read? What do they do when they read—take notes, annotate, discuss? How might you use online discussions to engage them in conversations about their reading?

3. How do you currently use media in your curriculum? What types of media do you use? What is the biggest hurdle you face in using media? How have your students responded to media? Where do you find it? Do you have resources you would recommend for quality media for other science teachers?

4. If you could introduce concepts online by embedding articles, lectures, demonstrations, and documentaries, how would you use class time to increase student engagement with the curriculum? What hands-on activities, labs, experiments, fieldwork, and/or creative activities would you like to do if you had more class time? How might introducing information online help your students better understand the content?

5. How would developing an online community with online discussions and group work make it possible to provide students with more opportunities to formulate hypotheses, design experiments, and collaborate on results? What strategies could you use to engage students in a more active role using online work and encourage them to be active participants in the science curriculum? How can online research and the integration of technology in general motivate students to solve problems and think critically about science topics?

6. How could you use your online space to facilitate online lab groups? How would you group students online? What benefits would you expect to see if students were able to discuss lab results online after class? How might these conversations positively impact lab reports that students produce?

7. How do you currently incorporate writing into your science curriculum? What challenges do you face when teaching writing? How might you address these challenges using a blended instruction approach to writing? How would the online space help you improve your writing program? How might writing more help your students better understand science? Brainstorm creative approaches to writing using a blended learning model.

8. How might you use online media tools to help students explore digital writing and multimedia projects to develop media literacy? Would you like to have students create documentaries using iMovie or create posters using Glogster to demonstrate an understanding of scientific topics? How would assigning multimedia projects inspire students to think more deeply about their work and the subject?

9

Math

The math standards place an emphasis on real-world problem solving, so the questions in this chapter are tied to real-world situations. This is a move away from standard textbook problems that have one correct answer. Instead students are encouraged to "make sense of problems and persevere in solving them" (Mathematics: Introduction: Standards for Mathematical Practice). In addition to anchoring these problems in the Common Core State Standards for each grade level, I have designed questions that invite dynamic discussions around the process of arriving at an answer. The Standards encourage students to "construct viable arguments and critique the reasoning of others" (Mathematics: Introduction: Standards for Mathematical Practice), which requires that they have time and space to communicate and collaborate. In life there are often a number of variables that must be considered, which means the answers to a given problem may vary. This variety lends itself to interesting conversations about the problems and the strategies different students use to solve them.

Online conversations require students to articulate their process, ask questions, offer insights, and build on other students' reasoning. This encourages them to approach math with a mental flexibility. Instead of looking for one right answer, these questions value the approach and process. This makes math less intimidating for students because the focus is no longer on getting the "right answer."

I have also incorporated elements of both argument and informative writing into these questions to encourage writing across the curriculum. Judy Willis (2011), former neurologist and teacher, asserts,

> When learning is examined through shared writing, students are exposed to multiple approaches to solving problems. This is so important in building the flexibility and open-minded approach. . . . Furthermore, students have the chance to communicate using their own words. They build communication skills they will surely use in their collaborations now and in the future science and math communities they will enter. (para. 9)

Dr. Willis highlights the importance of writing to support the brain's ability to take in, process, and retain concepts. She asserts that writing "can increase [students'] comfort with and success in understanding complex material, unfamiliar concepts, and subject-specific vocabulary" (para. 3). Since work done in online discussions must take the written form, this encourages students to explain their approach to math in writing, therefore fortifying their understanding of mathematical concepts.

Common Core State Standards: Upper Elementary Math

The following are the math standards addressed for the upper elementary level. I have also listed the Grades 4–5 writing standards because online work requires that students articulate their ideas in writing and publish them online.

Grades 4–5 Math Standards Addressed

4.NF.4	Apply and extend previous understandings of multiplication to multiply a fraction by a whole number. . . . Solve word problems involving multiplication of a fraction by a whole number, e.g., by using visual fraction models and equations to represent the problem.
5.G.2	Represent real-world and mathematical problems by graphing points in the first quadrant of the coordinate plane, and interpret coordinate values of points in the context of the situation.

Grades 4–5 Writing Standards Addressed

W.4-5.4	Produce clear and coherent writing in which the development and organization are appropriate to task, purpose, and audience.
W.4-5.6	With some guidance and support from adults, use technology, including the Internet, to produce and publish writing as well as to interact and collaborate with others.

Note: The language describing each standard is taken directly from the Common Core State Standards Initiative website: www.corestandards.org.

In fourth and fifth grade, the Standards state that students should focus on operations, algebraic thinking, fractions, measurements, and geometry. Though these questions focus on specific mathematical concepts, the question ideas can be applied to a variety of topics.

Example Online Activity 9.1. How Would Graphing Points on a Coordinate Plane Help Solve Real-World Problems?

Common Core Standards

5.G (Geometry)

The coordinate plane feels static and far removed from "real life," so this question challenges students to select a real-life circumstance and show how a coordinate plane can be used to problem solve. Students are able to choose a situation—astronomy, land use planning, or art—to think about in relation to the coordinate plane. By having several different topics to choose from, students can focus their energy on figuring out how the coordinate plane would be used in this situation. They must think about how charting points on a graph might be helpful to solving a problem in a given field. To do this, they have to consider how a chart would allow an astronomer, land use planner, or artist see relationships between points on the coordinate plane.

Weave Online Work Into the Classroom
With Student-Centered Activities

1. *Career Research.* As a class, brainstorm careers that use graphing on a regular basis. Once the class has generated a list, put students in

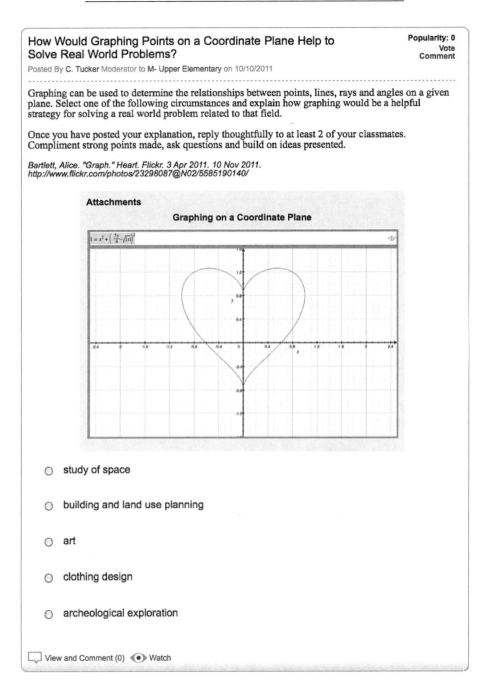

How Would Graphing Points on a Coordinate Plane Help to
Solve Real World Problems?

Popularity: 0
Vote
Comment

Posted By C. Tucker Moderator to M- Upper Elementary on 10/10/2011

Graphing can be used to determine the relationships between points, lines, rays and angles on a given plane. Select one of the following circumstances and explain how graphing would be a helpful strategy for solving a real world problem related to that field.

Once you have posted your explanation, reply thoughtfully to at least 2 of your classmates. Compliment strong points made, ask questions and build on ideas presented.

Bartlett, Alice. "Graph." Heart. Flickr. 3 Apr 2011. 10 Nov 2011.
http://www.flickr.com/photos/23298087@N02/5585190140/

Attachments

Graphing on a Coordinate Plane

○ study of space

○ building and land use planning

○ art

○ clothing design

○ archeological exploration

⬜ View and Comment (0)   ◉ Watch

small groups and assign a career to each group. Each career group researches how graphing is used in the job they are studying.

- What education is required for this job?
- What type of math must a person learn to work in this occupation?

- When would a person in this profession need to create and/or read graphs?
- Explain how graphs make their work easier or more successful.

This activity can be extended if each group creates a Lino canvas online (for more on Lino, see p. 126) where they post information about the career they researched. This can help students who are interested in math find out more about occupations that require math.

2. *Brainstorming.* In groups, ask students to think about graphs they have seen outside the classroom.

- What kinds of graphs do you see every day?
- What information do they provide?
- How is the graph display of information more helpful than if that information was written out?

Wall Wisher

www.wallwisher.com

Create a multimedia wall where students can brainstorm ideas, post notes, and attach files, pictures, music, and video.

Free

Be prepared to share the highlights of your discussion with the class. This brainstorm can take place in class or online using Wall Wisher.

3. *Creative Graphing Assignment.* Ask students to graph their home or school on a coordinate plane. Tell them to label the important points on the graph that represent key places, rooms, and objects in their home or at school. Make sure they use all four quadrants of the

National Center for Education Statistics Kids' Zone

nces.ed.gov/nceskids/createagraph/default.aspx

Create kid-friendly graphs (XY, bar, line, area, or pie).

Free

coordinate plane. Include an artistic component by asking them to draw small symbols or pictures to represent locations (e.g., bed to represent a bedroom at home, slice of pizza to symbolize the cafeteria at school). Students can also use the Kids' Zone graph creator available on the National Center for Education Statistics website.

Example Online Activity 9.2.
Design a Word Problem: Multiplying
Fractions to Solve Real-World Problems

Design a Word Problem: Multiplying Fractions to Solve Real World Problems

Popularity: 0
Vote
Comment

Posted By C. Tucker Moderator to M- Upper Elementary on 10/10/2011

Watch this Khan Academy explanation about multiplying fractions. Then think about your life and how you use fractions to solve real problems.

Design a word problem that requires your classmates to multiply fractions to solve a real world situation. Keep your language detailed and specific so your classmates can understand the problem that needs to be solved. Focus on a real word situation or dilemma.

Once you have posted your word problem, select a word problem designed by a peer and attempt to solve their word problem and explain your process. Post a reply to that person and address the following questions: How did you solve this problem? If you struggled to solve the problem, explain why. Was there information left out? Was the wording unclear?

Khan, Salman."Multiplying Fractions." Online video clip. Khan Academy. 7 Apr 2011. 17 Oct 2011
http://www.khanacademy.org/video/multiplying-fractions?playlist=Developmental+Math

Attachments

Khan Academy Tutorial

Multiplying Fractions

Multiply $\frac{5}{6} \cdot \frac{2}{3}$ Simplify your answer.

$$\frac{5}{6} \cdot \frac{2}{3} = \frac{5 \cdot 2}{6 \cdot 3} = \frac{10}{18} \cdot \frac{5}{9}$$

▶

Post a Comment

B	I	U	S	x_2	x^2	Ω	🔗	☰	☰	☰	☰	☰	☰	☰	☰

Post

Last 0 posts:

💬 View and Comment (0) 👁 Watch

Common Core Standards

4.NF (Number and Operations—Fractions)

This activity provides a Khan Academy video embedded into the discussion topic to support students' understanding of fractions. Khan Academy is a nonprofit education site with thousands of videos on a variety of academic topics. The videos are short tutorials led by Salman Khan, who explains concepts in a clear, easy-to-understand style. These videos can help support students when they are working at home and struggling with a concept. I highly recommend embedding the videos into discussion topics to differentiate instruction and engage students in conversations about the topics discussed in the tutorials.

> ### Khan Academy
>
> *www.khanacademy.org*
>
> Access thousands of videos on a variety of topics, including math, science, astronomy, art history, and test preparation. Students can also complete practice questions.
>
> Free

Once students have watched the Khan video (once, twice, three times depending on how much support they need), they must think about how they use fractions in their own lives and create a real-life problem involving fractions for their peers to solve. This activity can be applied to a variety of mathematical concepts. Because it requires that students apply the concept to their own lives, the teacher is freed from having to design a collection of real-life scenarios involving fractions. It also challenges students to consider carefully the problem and how they present that problem in writing so that it is clear and easy to understand.

Once students have posted their word problems, other students are able to critique any that are unclear or missing information. This is an incentive for students to take care designing and writing word problems that others can answer. Students must attempt to solve at least one of their peers' word problems and explain their process. This requires that they not only design an original problem but also practice solving one and explain in writing how they got their answer.

Weave Online Work Into the Classroom With Student-Centered Activities

1. *Group Strategy Session.* Have students share their best tips and/or strategies for solving word problems using their peers' word problems

Google Docs

docs.google.com

Create a shared Google doc for collaboration, or use Google forms to design a survey and collect information.

Free (gmail account needed)

as examples. Once they have shared tips, they can practice writing more complex word problems that require an additional step to solve. The class can add their tips and strategies to a shared Google doc, which they can add to throughout the year, creating a student-generated study guide.

Teacher's Note: Study Guides and Strategies is an education public service website that has a page titled "Solving Math Word Problems": www.studygs.net/mathproblems.htm.

Educreations

www.educreations.com

Create and share video lessons in minutes. The iPad app is an interactive whiteboard that records what students say and write. Images can also be uploaded into the virtual lesson.

Free

2. *Word Problem Challenge.* In groups, ask students to write another word problem about fractions (or a related topic) and exchange with another group. Students work together to solve the problem, then present the solution with a clear explanation to the class using a whiteboard or projector. If iPads are available, students could actually record their own student-produced videos, similar to Khan Academy tutorials, using Educreations.

ReadWriteThink

www.readwritethink.org/files/resources/ interactives/comic/index.html

Create cartoons and comics with images and thought bubbles to share or print.

Free

3. *Fraction Fun With Comic Strips.* In small groups, ask students to draw a comic strip representation of a word problem based on a real-life scenario, with each square focused on a step in the word problem. Encourage students to be creative with the characters, insert humor, and have fun with this! Students can use the online comic creator available from ReadWriteThink or design a comic Pixton (for more on Pixton, see p. 105).

Common Core State Standards: Middle School Math

The following are the math standards addressed for middle school. I have also listed the Grades 6–8 writing standards because online work requires that students articulate their ideas in writing and publish them online.

Grades 6–8 Math Standards Addressed

6.RP.1	Understand the concept of a ratio and use ratio language to describe a ratio relationship between two quantities.
7.SP.1	Understand that statistics can be used to gain information about a population by examining a sample of the population; generalizations about a population from a sample are valid only if the sample is representative of that population. Understand that random sampling tends to produce representative samples and support valid inferences.
7.SP.2	Use data from a random sample to draw inferences about a population with an unknown characteristic of interest. Generate multiple samples (or simulated samples) of the same size to gauge the variation in estimates or predictions.

Grades 6–8 Writing Standards Addressed

W.6-8.4	Produce clear and coherent writing in which the development and organization are appropriate to task, purpose, and audience.
W.6-8.6	With some guidance and support from adults, use technology, including the Internet, to produce and publish writing as well as to interact and collaborate with others.

Note: The language describing each standard is taken directly from the Common Core State Standards Initiative website: www.corestandards.org.

In sixth and seventh grades, the standards focus on ratios, proportions, the number system, expressions, equations, geometry, statistics, and probability. In eighth grade students also learn about functions. The scope of their study in each area develops each year to include more complex concepts and build on work done the previous year. As such the activities I designed for this section can be simplified for younger students (sixth) or made more complex for older students (eighth).

Example Online Activity 9.3.
Design a Survey, Take a Random Sampling, and Make a Generalization

Design a Survey, Take a Random Sampling & Make a Generalization

Popularity: 0
Vote
Comment

Posted By C. Tucker Moderator to M- Middle School on 10/10/2011

Tasks:
1. Design a short survey on a topic you are interested in. Your survey can take any format you prefer- questionnaire or interview; in person or online (e.g. http://www.surveymonkey.com).
2. Survey a random sampling of people.
3. Use your random sampling to make generalizations about how the larger population feels about your topic.

Written Response:
In your response begin by describing your survey. What was the topic of your survey? Why did you focus on this topic? What type of survey format did you use? Then explain how you ensured that you surveyed a "random" sampling of the population. Did you use a strategy to ensure your sampling was random? Are there any factors that might jeopardize the "random" nature of this sampling? What generalizations can you make based on the results of this survey. Use the data collected to support your generalizations.

Once you have posted your explanation, reply thoughtfully to at least 2 of your classmates. Compliment strong points made, ask questions and build on ideas presented.

"TV Viewing Template." Survey Monkey. www.surveymonkey.com

Attachments
Example Online Survey Using Survey Monkey

TV Viewing Template

1. How often do you watch television shows?
○ Extremely often
○ Very often
○ Moderately often
○ Slightly often
○ Not at all often

2. Out of all the television shows you have ever seen, which is your most favorite?

3. Out of all the television shows you have ever seen, which is your least favorite?

Post a Comment

B *I* U S x₂ x² Ω

Post

Last 0 posts:

View and Comment (0)   ●Watch

Common Core Standards

7.SP.1, 7.SP.2, W.6-8.4, W.6-8.6

This activity asks students to do a variety of different tasks to develop their understanding of statistics and probability. First, they must design a survey about a topic of interest to them; they

> **SurveyMonkey**
>
> *www.surveymonkey.com*
>
> Quickly create a survey, get feedback, and analyze the results.
>
> Free

can do this on paper or online. SurveyMonkey can be used to create and provide access to an online survey. Second, they must consider what a random sampling is and how it can be achieved. Third, they must collect survey responses and use the results to make some generalizations about the larger population.

Teachers immediately grab student interest when they ask students to design a survey on a topic of their choice; this creates immediate buy-in from students. With a class full of survey topics, results, and generalizations, this activity paves the way for countless follow-up discussions and debate opportunities.

Weave Online Work Into the Classroom With Student-Centered Activities

1. *Survey the Class.* Have students survey the entire class using the survey they designed for homework. Once everyone has taken the surveys, give students time to analyze the results. Have students discuss these questions in small groups:

- What were the results of the survey in class compared to the results of your previous random sampling?
- How did the opinions of your classmates differ from those of your random sampling?
- Were the generalizations you made based on your random sampling representative of the results you got from the class?
- How do you think the age of a population you survey impacts the results?

2. *Debate.* Ask students to debate the following questions:

- Is there such a thing as a truly random sampling? If so, how can this be achieved? If not, what barriers exist that are impossible to overcome?

- What factors impact the truthfulness of a survey?
- Under what conditions might a person you are surveying give a dishonest or inaccurate answer?
- How can this possible inaccuracy be eliminated or reduced?

Creately

creately.com

Create and collaborate on diagrams online. Drag and drop shapes, insert text, and use arrows to connect ideas. Share or export.

Create five free diagrams.

3. *Evaluating Trends in the U.S. Census.* Divide the class into small groups, and provide them with the results of the 2000 and 2010 U.S. Censuses. Ask the groups to identify key pieces of data to compare and analyze. What generalizations, patterns, and trends do they observe? What might be the importance of these patterns and trends? Students can chart the trends they observe using Creately, an online graph maker.

Teacher's Note: The U.S. Census Bureau (www.census.gov) has posted the census information for both 2000 and 2010.

Example Online Activity 9.4. Real-Life Ratios

Common Core Standards

6.RP.1, W.6-8.4, W.6-8.6

In sixth grade students must "understand ratio concepts and use ratio reasoning to solve problems" (Mathematics: Grade 6: Ratios and Proportional Relationships), then in seventh grade they must begin to "analyze proportional relationships" (Mathematics: Grade 7: Ratios and Proportional Relationships). To effectively move from understanding to analyzing proportional relationships, it is helpful to begin by asking students to discuss how they "see" and understand ratio relationships in their lives. That way they can begin to brainstorm real ratios they encounter and think about problems involving ratios in their lives.

I used the vote or suggest question structure in Collaborize Classroom to allow students to vote for their favorite example. This provides an incentive for students to be creative in their choices and carefully write their answers to ensure they are clear. If you are using a learning platform or learning management system without a voting feature, this activity can be done manually by asking students to select their favorite to share in class.

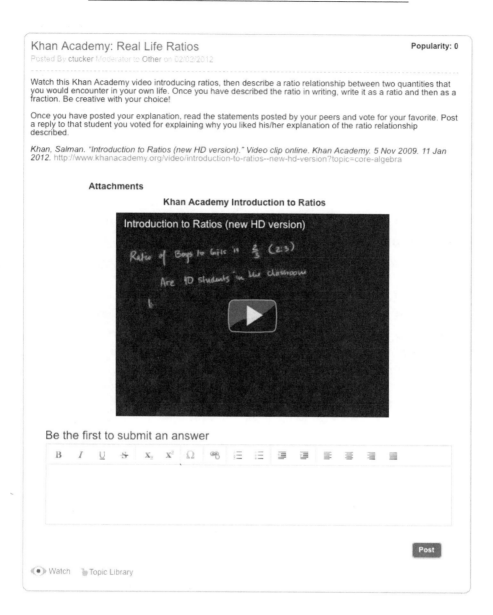

Khan Academy: Real Life Ratios   Popularity: 0
Posted By ctucker Moderator to Other on 02/02/2012

Watch this Khan Academy video introducing ratios, then describe a ratio relationship between two quantities that you would encounter in your own life. Once you have described the ratio in writing, write it as a ratio and then as a fraction. Be creative with your choice!

Once you have posted your explanation, read the statements posted by your peers and vote for your favorite. Post a reply to that student you voted for explaining why you liked his/her explanation of the ratio relationship described.

Khan, Salman. "Introduction to Ratios (new HD version)." Video clip online. Khan Academy. 5 Nov 2009. 11 Jan 2012. http://www.khanacademy.org/video/introduction-to-ratios--new-hd-version?topic=core-algebra

Attachments

Khan Academy Introduction to Ratios

Be the first to submit an answer

Watch   Topic Library

Weave Online Work Into the Classroom With Student-Centered Activities

1. *Observing Ratios in Life.* Divide the class into groups, and give each group a picture of a real-life situation. Students then brainstorm as many ratios as they can about the people and/or objects in the photo to share with the class. This could be facilitated as a timed game with groups competing to identify the most ratios in a given amount of time.

Teacher's Note: Google hosts the *Life* magazine photo archive, which has millions of historic photos teachers can use for this activity: images.google.com/hosted/life.

2. *Ratios in Cooking.* Ask students what meals or snacks they prepare at home. What ratios do they use? Have them write a recipe using ratios. This activity can culminate in a demonstration/presentation in which students prepare this dish in front of the class, explaining the ratios involved, or record a video of preparing this dish at home. This activity encourages students to make the connection between ratios and measurements. Students can post these recipes with photos on Pen.io (for more on Pen.io, see p. 128).

3. *Ratios in the Classroom.* Clear space in the classroom so students can comfortably move around and place a line down the center of the room. Then ask them to split based on gender, hair color, height, favorite sports, and so on. After each movement, ask them to observe the ratios in the room. Follow this activity with a discussion in small groups or a reflective writing assignment.

- What trends did the students notice?
- What generalizations can they make about the larger school population based on this activity?
- What did they realize about their classmates?

Common Core State Standards: High School Math

The following are the math standards addressed for high school. I have also listed the Grades 9–12 writing standards because online work requires that students articulate their ideas in writing and publish them online.

Grades 9–12 Math Standards Addressed

A-CED.1	Create equations and inequalities in one variable and use them to solve problems.
A-RED.1	Explain each step in solving a simple equation as following from the equality of numbers asserted at the previous step, starting from the assumption that the original equation has a solution. Construct a viable argument to justify a solution method.

| S-IC.1 | Understand statistics as a process for making inferences about population parameters based on a random sample from that population. |
| S-MD.5 | Weigh the possible outcomes of a decision by assigning probabilities to payoff values and finding expected values. |

Grades 9–12 Writing Standards Addressed

| W.9-12.4 | Produce clear and coherent writing in which the development and organization are appropriate to task, purpose, and audience. |
| W.9-12.6 | Use technology, including the Internet, to produce, publish, and update individual or shared writing products, taking advantage of technology's capacity to link to other information and to display information flexibly and dynamically. |

Note: The language describing each standard is taken directly from the Common Core State Standards Initiative website: www.corestandards.org.

The standards for high school are listed in categories by concept: number and quantity, algebra, functions, modeling, geometry, statistics, and probability. These mathematical concepts span multiple courses in Grades 9–12 and vary in complexity depending on the grade level.

Example Online Activity 9.5. Which Is More Dangerous—Men's Rugby or Women's Cheerleading?

Common Core Standards

S-IC.1, S-MD.5, W.9-12.4, W.9-12.6

This question requires students to use math modeling to link "classroom mathematics and statistics with everyday life, work, and decision-making" (Mathematics: High School: Modeling: Introduction). To answer the question students have to decide on the mathematical process and statistical information needed to solve this problem.

Real-world events and problems "are not organized and labeled for analysis; formulating tractable models . . . and analyzing them is appropriately a creative process" (Mathematics: High School:

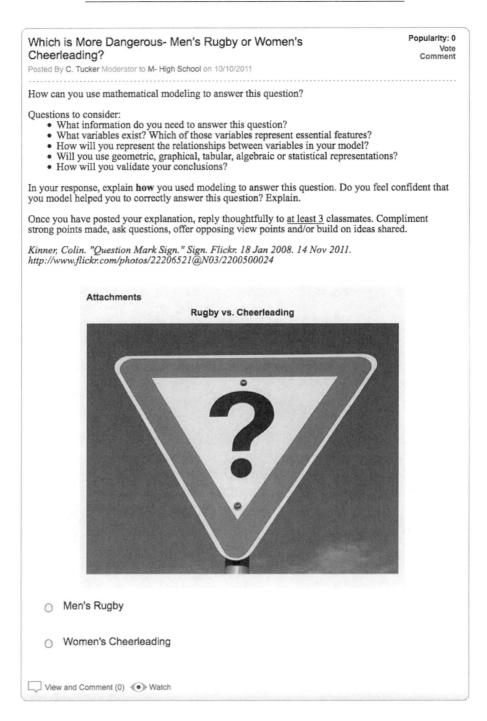

Which is More Dangerous- Men's Rugby or Women's Cheerleading?

Popularity: 0
Vote
Comment

Posted By C. Tucker Moderator to M- High School on 10/10/2011

How can you use mathematical modeling to answer this question?

Questions to consider:
- What information do you need to answer this question?
- What variables exist? Which of those variables represent essential features?
- How will you represent the relationships between variables in your model?
- Will you use geometric, graphical, tabular, algebraic or statistical representations?
- How will you validate your conclusions?

In your response, explain **how** you used modeling to answer this question. Do you feel confident that you model helped you to correctly answer this question? Explain.

Once you have posted your explanation, reply thoughtfully to at least 3 classmates. Compliment strong points made, ask questions, offer opposing view points and/or build on ideas shared.

Kinner, Colin. "Question Mark Sign." Sign. Flickr. 18 Jan 2008. 14 Nov 2011.
http://www.flickr.com/photos/22206521@N03/2200500024

Attachments

Rugby vs. Cheerleading

○ Men's Rugby

○ Women's Cheerleading

View and Comment (0) Watch

Modeling: Introduction). This creative element requires that students ask questions, conduct research to locate necessary data, identify significant variables, and consider a variety of approaches to problem solving. In addition to using mathematical modeling to answer the question, students must clearly report "on the conclusions and reasoning behind them" in writing (Mathematics: High School: Modeling: Introduction). Because they must select the sport they believe is most dangerous and justify their answer with evidence and analysis, this also has an element of argument writing.

Weave Online Work Into the Classroom With Student-Centered Activities

1. *Group Discussion.* Divide the class into small groups to discuss the following questions:

- What strategies do you use when you come across a problem you cannot solve?
- How do you cope with not having enough information to solve a problem?
- How can learning to deal with problems that seem impossible help you solve difficult word problems?
- Why is it crucial to have strategies to solve problems when dealing with real-life situations?

Once they have had a conversation about these questions, ask students to create a helpful tips poster with their strategies for problem solving that they can post in the classroom. This can also be done online with a creative tool like Glogster (for more on Glogster, see p. 93).

2. *Group Challenge.* In small groups, students write a word problem based on a real-life situation with a piece of missing information and then exchange with another group. The groups work together to solve the problem despite the missing piece of information. After they have attempted to solve their problem, they explain their process with the class.

3. *Creative Assignment.* Divide the class into small groups, and present them with a real-life problem to be solved (e.g., designing the layout of the booths for Club Awareness Day, creating an emergency plan for the school to evacuate quickly and effectively during a fire, analyzing the possible risks to students on campus). Ask them to show their process using a flowchart with images to represent the problem, variables, relationship between variables, operations, results, and conclusions. They then present this visual to the class and explain how they solved the problem. Students can also create an online flowchart using Gliffy (for more on Gliffy, see p. 111).

Example Online Activity 9.6. Algebra: How Much Is College Going to Cost You?

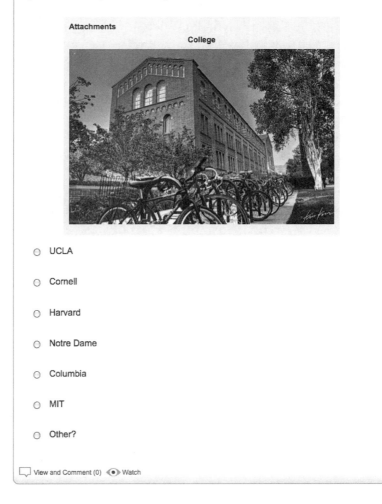

Algebra: How Much is College Going To Cost You?

Posted By C. Tucker Moderator to M- High School on 11/14/2011

Popularity: 0
Vote
Comment

Choose a college from the list below that you would like to attend. Research the tuition for that college.

- How much will it cost to attend this school for a year?
- How much has tuition increased each year on average?
- What is the standard rate for a student loan?
- How long will it take you to pay off your student loan?

Complete the necessary research on your chosen college and identify the variables present, then write this problem as an algebraic equation. Under the algebraic expression, explain your process, discuss what you found out during your research, and identify the variables present in your equation.

Once you have posted your equation, read the equations posted by your peers and reply thoughtfully to <u>at least 3</u> other students. Compliment strong points, ask questions and build on ideas shared!

Kros, Kris. "Campus Bikes." Bikes. Flickr. 24 Oct 2007. 14 Nov 2011
http://www.flickr.com/photos/37369621@N00/2571971105/

Attachments

College

○ UCLA

○ Cornell

○ Harvard

○ Notre Dame

○ Columbia

○ MIT

○ Other?

View and Comment (0) ◉ Watch

Common Core Standards

A-CED.1, A-RED.1, W.9-12.4, W.9-12.6

The rising cost of college is a hot topic in education, and it is a subject of interest to many students considering postsecondary studies. This question presents students with a multistep problem. To solve the problem and answer the question, they must apply their understanding of algebra.

First, students must select a college to research. They need to find out the yearly tuition for that school and then factor in the rate at which the tuition is increasing on average each year. They must also find out how much time the average undergraduate spends at that school before earning his or her degree.

Once students have done this preliminary research, they have to research college loans and determine how long it would take to pay off their loan if they attended this school for X (number of years) at an annual rate of Y (cost of tuition per year) factoring in Z (the rate of increase in tuition per year). Then they take that number and determine how long it would take to pay off a standard student loan for the cost of their college degree.

For many students not only does this question deal with a topic they care about, but the information they find during their research will be important to consider as they progress in school.

Weave Online Work Into the Classroom With Student-Centered Activities

1. *Class Discussion.* In small groups, ask students to discuss the following questions and then be prepared to discuss as a whole class:

- Were you surprised by the cost of tuition?
- Do you think the cost of college is worth the benefits?
- What are the benefits of attending a 4-year college or university?

This could also be extended into another research assignment and discussion.

Teacher's Note: The Pew Research Center, a nonpartisan fact tank, released a report in May 2011 titled "Is College Worth It?" This would make an interesting addition to the discussion of college, the costs associated with earning a degree, and the benefits of having a degree in today's job market. A summary of the report is available at

pewresearch.org/pubs/1993/survey-is-college-degree-worth-cost
-debt-college-presidents-higher-education-system.

2. *Cutting College Costs.* Ask students to research their "safety school" to see if it is a better deal than the school they initially researched. Have them compare the two schools and brainstorm ways they could cut costs. What is the price of housing? Is there an alternative place to live near the campus that would be cheaper? What does a meal plan cost? Could you work part time? If so, what would you do for work, how many hours could you reasonably work a week, and what would a realistic income be? How could saving money or earning money help you manage the cost of college without incurring huge debt? Ask students to present their findings in small groups.

3. *Interest Rates Activity.* Have students graph how much money they would owe if they paid off their student loan in 5, 10, 15, or 20 years. (*Note:* Students should use the total cost of college they calculated from the online activity.) Their graphs should visually show the difference in total costs for each year marker. Ask them to consider the following questions:

- How much would your payments change if you paid off your student loan earlier?
- How much money could you save if you paid off your loan in 10 years versus 20 years?
- What did this exercise teach you about interest?

Students should be prepared to share their charts with the class. Students can create their charts using Gliffy (for more on Gliffy, see p. 111) or Creately (for more on Creately, see p. 174).

Chapter Summary

The math standards identify key areas of focus per grade level from kindergarten through eighth grade. Each year the math concepts build on the work done the previous year. Mathematical concepts become increasingly complex as students move through school. Because students move from a general to a more specific understanding of these ideas, it is critical that they have a solid foundation on which to build. Providing students with a space to discuss, describe, analyze, question, collaborate, and problem solve makes it possible for them to understand challenging mathematical concepts.

The high school standards identify key conceptual categories of study that students need in order to be prepared for life beyond high school: number and quantity, algebra, functions, modeling, geometry, statistics, and probability. These areas of study span multiple courses and build on the foundation created in Grades K–8.

Incorporating online discussions and group work into the traditional math curriculum takes math from solitary practice to collaborative effort. Students have a support network of peers they can talk with about problems they encounter. It also makes it easier for teachers to present students with real-life scenarios and problems that they need to solve. This need to make tangible connections between math concepts and real life is stressed throughout the Standards.

In this chapter I have designed two online math problems with real-life relevance for each level: upper elementary, middle school, and high school. These activities engage students in problem solving and collaboration. They include media to grab student interest and make abstract concepts more concrete. These activities can be made simpler or more complex depending on your student population.

Book Study Questions

1. How do you make math relevant for your students? What connections do you make between math and real-life situations that impact your students? Is it a challenge to connect the math curriculum to topics that interest your students? How can the integration of technology into your math curriculum increase student interest?

2. How do you currently support the development of reading and writing in your math curriculum? What do students typically read? What do they do when they read from their text—take notes, annotate, discuss? How might you use online discussions to engage them in conversations about their math reading?

3. What are the benefits of teaching writing in math? How do you currently incorporate writing into your math curriculum? What challenges do you face teaching writing in math? How might you address these challenges using a blended instruction approach to writing? How would the online space help you improve your writing program? How might writing more help your students better understand math? Brainstorm creative approaches to writing using a blended learning model.

4. How do you currently use media in your curriculum? What types of media do you use? What is the biggest hurdle you face in using media? How have your students responded to media? Where do you find it? Do you have resources you would recommend for quality media for other math teachers?

5. If you could introduce concepts online by embedding lectures, video tutorials, and demonstrations, how would you use your time in the classroom to increase student engagement with the curriculum? What hands-on activities, creative assignments, experiments, and fieldwork would you like to do if you had more class time? How might introducing information online help your students better understand the content?

6. How would developing an online community with online discussions and group work make it possible to provide students with more opportunities to formulate questions, design word problems, and collaborate on results? What strategies could you use to engage students in a more active role using online work to encourage them to be active participants in the math curriculum? How can online research and the integration of technology in general motivate students to problem solve and think critically about math topics?

7. How could you use your online space to facilitate online math study groups? How would you group students online? What benefits would you expect to see if students were able to discuss mathematical concepts online after class? How might these conversations positively impact their comprehension and engagement?

8. Why is it beneficial for students to design problems? How does asking students to design real-life problems force them to understand mathematical concepts? How can the online space be leveraged to give students more opportunities to design questions, problems, and challenges for their peers to solve?

Reference

Willis, J. (2011). The brain-based benefits of writing for math and science learning. *Edutopia*. Retrieved from http://www.edutopia.org/blog/writing-executive-function-brain-research-judy-willis

10

Flip Your Instruction With Online Discussions

What Is the Flipped Classroom?

The term *flipped classroom* refers to a course in which the instructor delivers a percentage of the content online outside of class. The concept of the flipped classroom (also known as *reverse instruction*) explores the ways technology integration can be used to provide teachers with more flexibility and time in their classrooms. There has been a surge of interest in this model at the middle school and high school level over the last academic year. Teachers are recording their lectures and posting them on YouTube and TeacherTube for students to watch at home to replace traditional homework assignments. The purpose of flipping instruction is to free up class time so it can be used more effectively to group students together to practice and problem solve—maximizing the potential of the group in the physical classroom.

In the traditional teaching paradigm delivery of content takes place within the walls of the classroom. Homework is usually an extension of that work, which requires students to review and apply the information they learned in class. In this model students are isolated at home during the practice phase of learning, which often requires the most coaching, correction, and collaboration to be effective. When students are asked to complete practice problems or read out of a textbook at home, there is no subject area expert who can answer questions, provide clarity, or guide students in their work. This task often falls to a parent who may not have the subject area knowledge or expertise, the language proficiency, or the time to help. This model sets up struggling students to fail because they have no support to help them be successful. Even the most motivated and diligent students can become frustrated and disillusioned during this phase of learning if they do not feel they have the necessary support to work through the tasks assigned.

There is a national debate taking place about the value of homework. Many argue that homework is too time consuming and does not improve student success in school. Maybe the real question is this: How can we transform homework to ensure it is valuable for students and directly impacts their success in the classroom?

A growing number of teachers feel it is a poor use of class time to have students silently taking notes, when they could be working together in small learning communities. When instruction is flipped, class time can be used to support group work, labs and experiments, or application practice. As Jerry Overmyer (n.d.), of the University of Northern Colorado, defines it

> the flipped classroom model encompasses any use of using Internet technology to leverage the learning in your classroom, so you can spend more time interacting with students instead of lecturing. This is most commonly being done using teacher created videos (aka vodcasting) that students view outside of class time. (para. 2)

For many teachers, time limits their ability to provide both the necessary content-specific information and engage students in meaningful activities in the classroom. This frustrates many teachers who realize that the hands-on application is a critical step in progressing up Bloom's pyramid beyond simply remembering to analyze, synthesize, evaluate, and create. Accessing these higher-order thinking skills requires that students work with the information provided to make sense of it. Maximizing the collective potential of the group during this phase of learning with collaborative group work makes it more effective and meaningful.

Ramsey Musallam, EdD, a dynamic chemistry teacher who regularly flips his instruction, defines flipped teaching as "leveraging technology to appropriately pair the learning activity with the learning environment. Activity refers to the cognitive requirement associated with the task, and environment refers to whether the task takes place in classroom community or an individual setting" (personal communication, March 2012). I love this definition because Musallam makes an important point about the value of matching the type of learning activity with the optimal setting or environment to achieve the best results for students. Often when concepts are explained, it is easier for a student to work independently and at his or her own pace. When students are practicing a skill or applying knowledge, it is ideal to have a supportive community to work with and a subject area expert present to help guide them. Flipping instruction allows a teacher to transfer knowledge to students via media online, while using class time to engage the group in practice. This way students have a support network of peers with whom they can ask questions, problem solve, and collaborate.

"Homework" in the Flipped Classroom Model

Using an online learning platform with the ability to embed media and a discussion component makes it possible for a teacher to present documents, images/photos, and videos online for students to view, take notes on, and discuss. Presenting information online for homework and then using class time to apply, analyze, synthesize, evaluate, and create ensures that the teacher is present when students are being asked to demonstrate higher-order thinking skills.

Presenting information inside the frame of a discussion question can make this reverse model of instruction even more effective because students must think more deeply about the content to discuss it with their peers. Consider the example below that instructs students to view an embedded Khan Academy video on the phases of meiosis and then discuss a particular phase in detail.

If a teacher asks students to simply view the Khan Academy video to prepare for a lab, the amount of information retained will be lower than if they are also asked to answer a discussion question about the video. If the teacher embeds the video into a discussion question that asks students to choose one phase in the process to describe in detail, then they will have applied what they learned and remember more of what they heard. This also allows them to

Take a Closer Look at the Phases of Meiosis

Posted By **Catlin** Moderator to **Example Questions** on 11/15/2011

Popularity: 0
Vote
Comment

Choose a stage to explain in detail. Explain the significance of the prefix's meaning in relation to this stage of cell reproduction. Reply to <u>at least 2</u> peers.

Attachments

"Stages of Meiosis" from Khan Academy

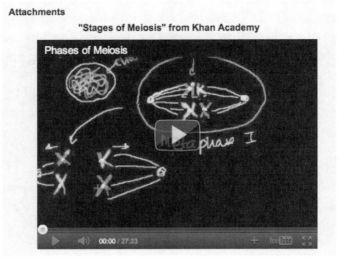

concentrate on the aspect of this scientific process they understand best. Then they can read what their peers have written about the other phases of meiosis that they may not understand as clearly. This sets up students to become resources for one another in the learning process. The homework becomes an interactive experience with the other members of the class instead of a solitary practice.

Discussion questions can vary in difficulty depending on the ability of the students. Basic discussion questions might ask students to summarize the main points of the lecture, while more complex questions might ask students to apply or make connections between concepts. Tailoring the questions to the student population and giving students a degree of freedom in how they answer a question makes it possible for teachers to more easily differentiate their instruction and curriculum to challenge the higher-level students while supporting the lower-level students.

An online discussion question paired with a video or lecture engages the community of learners in conversation. Students are encouraged to use each other as resources in discussions about the video or lecture content. If a student is struggling with an aspect of the online lecture or video, her or she has a space to ask questions, receive peer and/or instructor guidance, and read what classmates have to say without waiting for the next class. This creates a 24-hour support network for students.

Teachers using online discussions can flip their classrooms and introduce concepts at home to maximize valuable class time and increase student engagement. This addition to the lecture also engages the community of inquiry outside of the classroom to problem solve and discuss issues related to the content.

Strategies for Flipping Instruction

1. Embed a video lecture or tutorial video into a discussion question. Ask students to watch the video lecture, take notes, and discuss. In class, students use the information presented online to work in collaborative groups to apply or practice the concepts, complete a lab or experiment, debate an issue, or discuss the information.

Do you agree with Noam Chomsky's message about President Obama?

Popularity: 0
Vote
Comment

Posted By Catlin Moderator to 2A Discussion Qs on 08/22/2011

Support your position with a clear explanation and strong evidence. Reply thoughtfully to <u>at least 2</u> peers.

YES

NO

Attachments

Noam Chomsky Lecture at Trinity College

2. Ask students to view a clip from a debate, documentary, or news story, then take a position on the topic in a yes/no question and justify that position with evidence and a clear explanation. Then follow this online debate with a live in-class debate.

Does the U.S. government have a responsibility to lead the global reduction of carbon emissions?

Popularity: 0
Vote
Comment

Posted By Catlin Moderator to P1 Discussion Qs on 11/16/2011

Vote yes or no, then present a clear claim about whether or not you think the United States should be a leader in the reduction of carbon emissions. Support your claim with evidence and analysis.

YES

NO

Attachments

Al Gore Speaking to Congress on Global Warming

3. Ask students to research and discuss a topic online for homework, then present findings in a presentation in class. This strategy frees the teacher from needing to lecture in class and instead requires students to become the experts and find credible information on a given topic.

Expert Groups: The Plague and Other Illnesses in Elizabethan England

Popularity: 0
Vote
Comment

Posted By Catlin Moderator to Example Questions on 11/28/2011

In your group research this topic. Your job as a member of this group is to find at least 2 strong online resources to share with the other 3-4 members of your group. Discuss the information you found to ensure you understand it. Ask questions, make comments, identify information that surprised you, compliment peers on strong resources, etc.

In class Wednesday you will be responsible for compiling your BEST information to create an interesting presentation.

Throm, C. "The Plague Doctor." [Graphite and Watercolor]. *The Art of CC Throm*. Retrieved from http://www.ccthrom.com/image_code/fantasy_page01.html

Attachments

Black Death Doctor

Although most teachers think they must record their lectures to flip their instruction, I often encourage teachers to think outside the box when it comes to flipping instruction. If you are camera shy or don't have the equipment or technology to record and post videos, then flip other types of media.

There are documentaries available for teachers who want to expose students to a historical time period, important people and events, or moments in history. History.com and PBS.org are fabulous resources for these types of videos. Teachers can show TED talks, interviews with famous people, authors reading their work, news clips on current events, and so on. There is so much recorded video content available on the Web that can easily be embedded into an online discussion topic.

Photographs, images, artwork, and flowcharts can be embedded into the online space for students to view at length and discuss. When images are projected in class, students rarely have the necessary time to appreciate the nuances and discuss the importance of those images.

Documents are another form of media that can be used in the online space to flip instruction. I often embed articles, biographies, interview transcripts, and written notes online for students to read at their own pace and then discuss. In-class reading takes time, requires countless photocopies, and gives some students anxiety. When they are able to take their time, read at their own pace, then discuss information with their peers, they are more likely to comprehend what they have read and apply that information.

Ultimately, a teacher can flip any transfer of knowledge that takes substantial class time by making that information available online. Pairing that information with a discussion, debate, group assignment, or task engages higher-order thinking and improves retention.

What Happens in the Flipped Classroom?

In a flipped classroom model, in-class time is used to introduce a given concept with an inquiry-based activity that engages students and excites interest in the topic. This inquiry-based activity can be used to identify previous knowledge, brainstorm questions, and/or engage students in exploring a concept that has not yet been explained. Then the teacher transfers knowledge or information to the students via media viewed online outside of class.

After content has been viewed at home and discussed online, it is critical that the teacher weave that online information back into the physical classroom with student-centered activities. Students should be asked to directly apply what they learned online during the next class to reinforce their understanding of the information. It also provides an incentive for students to prioritize that work done online since it directly impacts their ability to be successful in class. Designing in-class activities that build on information presented online is a necessary step in successfully flipping the traditional classroom. If students have been presented with information at home, then in class they should work with their peers to cement that knowledge by engaging their higher-order thinking skills.

For example, if students watch a History.com documentary on the Great Depression at home and discuss it online with their peers, then a teacher can use class time to organize students into collaborative groups to produce a newspaper from that time period that includes several articles focused on a variety of topics from the job market to sports and entertainment to government programs. This requires that students work together using what they have learned to make it more real and relevant. This model requires that students develop and use 21st century skills such as communication and collaboration both online and in person.

How Can I Lesson Plan for the Flipped Classroom Model?

Every teacher has his or her own approach to lesson planning. Because the flipped classroom model is new to many teachers, I want to share the strategy I use for designing a complete flipped classroom lesson. I have created a simple chart (see Resource 10.1) that I use when designing my flipped lessons. I begin by identifying the inquiry-based activity I want to use to introduce a given topic and pique student interest. Then I decide on the media and discussion question I want to present online. Finally, I plan a student-centered activity that requires students to apply their knowledge and demonstrate higher-order thinking.

What If Students Don't Do Their Homework?

Whenever I present on the topic of the flipped classroom model, teachers ask me what I do when a student does not complete the work assigned online. They bring up a valid concern. How can a student who did not view the content at home engage in student-centered in-class activities that build on that online work?

Resource 10.1   Design a Flipped Lesson

Inquiry-Driven Activity (in the classroom) ⟹	Transfer Knowledge and Pair With Discussion or Activity (at home) ⟹	Student-Centered Extension Activity (in the classroom)
Common State Standards Addressed:		

There is no perfect answer to this question. In an ideal world, all students complete their homework. In reality, there are always a few who do not do their homework. I have handled this situation in one of two ways.

The first time I flipped my classroom, I had approximately five to six students in each period come to class without viewing the online content. I provided them with an article on the same topic and had them read and annotate the article, then write a summary quietly in the back section of the classroom while the rest of the students did a creative hands-on activity. I could tell many of the kids reading the article were curious about what their peers were doing in groups.

After that I decided to make my in-class activities as creative as possible to motivate students to complete the online work. I figured they would be more invested in the homework if they thought they would get to do something fun with their peers in class. The next time I flipped my classroom I had only one to three students come unprepared. One student commented to a peer, "She's going to make us learn this either way, so I might as well get to watch it online and talk about it with everyone."

Another strategy that I ended up using more frequently was to have the students who did not complete the homework observe the groups as they worked and take notes. This allowed them to benefit from the dialogue and exchanges of their peers without getting to be an active participant, which was frustrating and a good incentive to complete the homework in the future. I asked that they submit their notes to me at the end of the period so they would get participation points despite being unprepared. I found this was even more effective in motivating students to complete their homework because they were intrigued by the work they had observed in the previous class.

Each teacher needs to decide on a method for managing students who have not completed their homework in a flipped model. If you have technology in your classroom, students can view the online content while their peers complete activities. However, if you do not have technology, one of the strategies I described above may help you manage those students who come to class unprepared. I found that the second strategy, which required them to observe, actually saved me time because I did not have to find and make copies of a comparable text version of the online content. These are not the only strategies a teacher can use, but I found success with them.

Tips for Successfully Flipping Your Classroom

"Don't Reinvent the Wheel"

This cliché—though tired—is very appropriate for teachers attempting to deliver information online. If you have a lecture on a topic that you want to share with your students online, check that the subject has not already been explained and recorded by another teacher or professor and captured on YouTube EDU, SchoolTube, TeacherTube, or iTunes U.

As this concept of the flipped classroom becomes more popular, the already vast number of resources online will continue to grow.

Check online before you invest your time and energy in recording a lecture or series of them.

Break Up Online Lecture

If you present information online, it is still important to break up the task so that students are not listening to and taking notes on an extended lecture. Instead, break up the lecture into 5–10-minute intervals or ask them to pause the recording to complete a task, engage in an online discussion, or complete an exercise. If you are recording your own lectures, it will be easy to break them up into mini-recordings to ensure the segments are not too long. If you are using another educator's lectures, then instruct students when to stop the video. For example, you can ask them to pause a video recording at 5:11 and post a response to the first discussion question or complete an activity before progressing in the lecture. Just make sure all directions are clear so students know when to pause and what to do. The beauty of presenting information in a recorded lecture is that students are in control of the play button. They can stop, pause, and replay. Make use of that flexibility!

Check for Understanding With a Variety of Assessments in Class

It is important to make sure students have *actually* watched the lecture or video they have been asked to view online for homework. Some teachers choose to give short quizzes, while others check student notes. It is crucial that students know the information presented will be critical to their success in class. At the start of this new format, quizzing students to emphasize the importance of their work done at home may be the incentive they need to complete the homework task.

Long term, students will be more likely to complete their homework if they know they will need the information to effectively engage with their peers in class. Teachers who consistently build in class on concepts presented online at home with activities that ask students to apply what they learned and to problem solve will effectively cultivate a community of inquiry that is student centered. The focus of work done in the flipped classroom is all about the students. Instead of listening to a teacher lecture at the front of the room, students work together and the teacher circulates, assisting, and guiding as needed.

The following are idea charts to inspire creative online delivery of content and collaborative in-class tasks that build on information presented online. These offer suggestions, by subject, for how teachers can embed media online and build on that work with fun in-class activities to maximize collaboration and engagement.

English

Media-Embedded Ideas	Weave Online Work Into Class
• Clips of a movie version of a novel to compare/contrast with actual text • Documentaries related to the historical time period of a novel • Lectures on English topics (e.g., Shakespeare's sonnets, evolution of English language) • Music related to a novel (time period and/or theme) • Videos to prompt or inspire responses/creative writing • Recorded readings of novel excerpts and poetry • Watch a video clip and analyze rhetorical devices • Watch poetry performed	• Debate whether the book or movie version is better. • Act out a scene in class that they watched at home. • Work together to write an original short story or poem in collaborative groups. • In groups students discuss a piece of writing and analyze it for strong elements based on the lecture they listened to online. • Recite a poem—memorized or original slam poem. • Recreate a scene from a Shakespeare play using modern dialogue, then upload.

History/Social Studies

Media-Embedded Ideas	Weave Online Work Into Class
• Lectures on historical topics • Live debates—analyze bias present and/or positions stated • Presidential speeches • Student-produced newscasts about a current event • Clips of news stories on important events evaluated for accuracy and/or bias • Documentaries and/or audio recordings of famous speeches • Propaganda videos (e.g., from World War II, Cold War)—What ideologies, doctrines, or stereotypes are present? How do they affect you as a viewer?	• Reenact a battle or trench warfare. • Debate an issue in class. • Enact the feudal system with students assuming the roles of people in different social classes. • Create a French Revolution board game that includes the different events of Napoleon's rise to and fall from power. • Assume the identity of a country in Europe (ethnic ties and tensions, culture, priorities) to demonstrate the creation of alliances during World War I. • Film a political movie or design a piece of political propaganda. • Write a newspaper with a variety of articles from the Great Depression.

Science

Media-Embedded Ideas	Weave Online Work Into Class
• Videos of experts/lectures • Scientific videos and/or documentaries • Demonstrations and/or filmed lab experiments • Debates on controversial topics (e.g., cloning) • News clips on key scientific issues	• Build a model of a DNA strand or a cell structure. • Conduct a lab/hands-on experiment. • Design a lab experiment with lab groups to test a theory. • Gather specimens and/or materials needed for labs in nature. • Debate scientific issues in class.

Math

Media-Embedded Ideas	Weave Online Work Into Class
• Lectures and/or demonstrations • TED talks on math topics (www.ted.com) • Homework "help" videos • Online lessons/tutorials • Teacher- or student-produced how-to videos on mathematical processes • Clip of a poker game to evaluate probability and statistics • Clip of a cooking show to demonstrate importance of measurement	• Take photographs from life that present mathematical concepts and/or real-life problems that need to be solved. • Build a scale model or Lego reconstruction of a building using the proper proportions and measurements. • Conduct labs and hands-on experiments to demonstrate mathematical concepts. • Conduct a class survey to demonstrate statistical significance. • Test probability and statistics during an in-class casino event. • Make a dish using a detailed recipe involving measurements. • Create a detailed itinerary for a trip on a budget. • Cost a construction project of your "dream home."

Some educators have criticized the flipped classroom model, arguing that it is a "virtual sage on the stage." When only asked to watch a lecture or video online, students still receive the information passively. However, when media is coupled with dynamic discussion questions, creative tasks, and group work using an online discussion platform, students become actively engaged.

The point is to inspire students to actively interact with information, work with their peers to construct meaning, and demonstrate higher-order thinking skills. All of this can be accomplished when flipped instruction takes place in conjunction with meaningful tasks and conversations.

This argument against the flipped classroom also fails to appreciate the work done in class, which is more student centered than in a traditional classroom. In class, students work together to accomplish tasks and the teacher can act as a one-on-one tutor, addressing issues and answering questions to further differentiate and personalize instruction.

Teachers interested in flipping their classroom should keep in mind that it does not have to happen every day. In fact, the classroom can be flipped occasionally depending on the content being covered. It is just another way to leverage the online space and technology to be more effective!

Below is an example of the information flow in a flipped instruction model.

Chapter Summary

Flipped classroom refers to a model of instruction in which information that has been traditionally delivered in class via lecture is instead presented online and viewed at home by students for homework. When paired with dynamic discussion questions and online activities using an online discussion platform, this method of delivering information can be even more effective. Students can engage with their peers online to discuss concepts, ask questions, and demonstrate higher-level thinking. When information is presented online at home via lecture, videos, documentaries, and so on, there is more time in class for students to work together in collaborative groups to apply what they have learned in fun and creative ways. Teachers can use this model to create student-centered activities that require communication and collaboration—necessary components of a community of inquiry.

Book Study Questions

1. How much time do you spend each day and/or week presenting information? When you present information, what methods do you typically use—lecture, videos, reading from books? How do your students respond to your methods of delivering information? Do they prefer one style over another?

2. How well do you think the flipped model of instruction would work for your subject area and/or student population? How do you think your students would respond to watching a lecture or video at home?

3. What kinds of media do you already use in your class? How challenging would it be to present that information online? Do you have any favorite websites where you find videos?

4. If you spent less time lecturing in class, what would you love to do with that extra time? For example, what kinds of collaborative group work would you enjoy facilitating? How might collaborative group work and student-driven projects motivate students to think deeply or engage actively in the class?

5. What challenges do you think you might encounter flipping your classroom? Would producing your own videos be an obstacle? Would it be hard to find the content you need online? Do you think this model would be more or less time consuming compared to the way you teach now?

6. How might pairing videos and/or lectures with discussion questions help improve retention and engagement?

7. What types of questions would you design to complement the online videos you are asking students to view? What kinds of conversations would inspire students to actively engage in discussions? What activities and/or tasks might you ask students to complete in relation to the work presented online to inspire higher-level thinking?

8. How would you assess students in class to ensure they were viewing the lectures, videos, documentaries, etc.? If students were watching subject-specific content at home and engaging in online discussions, would this reduce the amount of paperwork you grade? How could this model be used to replace and/or improve what you already do?

9. What benefits do you think flipping instruction would have on student interest, engagement, responsibility, and/or focus?

10. How might using this flipped model of instruction make it easier for you to differentiate and customize your curriculum to better meet the needs of all students?

Reference

Overmyer, J. (n.d.). *Vodcasting and the flipped classroom.* Retrieved from http://mast.unco.edu/programs/flipped/

11

Assessing
Work Online

Many teachers have asked me how I assess student work online. The culture of testing in education has conditioned teachers to constantly question how they will assess and evaluate the work students do. Traditionally, teachers collect homework, grade it, record those grades, then return the work to the students. This process is time consuming for teachers, especially those who assign written homework every night.

The time it takes to give feedback and return papers can make this process ineffective because by the time edited assignments are returned, the class has moved on. Unless students are being asked to revisit that work, it rarely gets more than a cursory glance when students check the point value then toss it in a backpack.

There is also immense pressure on teachers to make the work assigned meaningful (not "busy work") and to provide specific feedback. This is a lot to ask of teachers who are seeing their class sizes soar. The student-to-teacher ratio is growing and making it more challenging for teachers to design a variety of meaningful assessments and provide timely feedback.

Technology has the potential to shift the way work is done, how students engage with each other, and how teachers evaluate and assess the work done. Leveraging technology successfully to save time, reduce paperwork, and engage students in more meaningful activities requires that teachers embrace the following truths about 21st century learning:

1. *Teachers do not need to grade everything.* I remember being in credential school and my mentor teacher told me that if I was reading and grading everything, then my students were not doing enough writing. It took me 5 years of teaching to accept this reality. With a ratio of 164 students to me, I realized how unrealistic it was for me to try to evaluate and grade everything. The energy and time I put into grading daily homework assignments was keeping me from experimenting with new teaching techniques, designing new activities and creative projects, and reflecting on and improving my own teaching practices.

2. *Students are valuable resources in the classroom.* Students have the potential to be a powerful support network for one another. Teaching them to engage with each other and provide meaningful feedback can take the pressure off the teacher to be the sole source of information in the classroom. Peer editing and critiquing can be extremely effective, but it requires scaffolding from the teacher in the early stages. The payoff is a room full of students who automatically ask each other questions before they seek help from their teacher.

3. *Grades are not always the most motivating factor.* Although many students are concerned about their grade in a class, appealing to students' interest, highlighting the real-world relevance of work assigned, showing them that their work is directly impacting the class, and helping them recognize their own growth are more powerful long-term incentives.

4. *More writing leads to better writing.* The more teachers across all disciplines can get students writing, the more writing will improve. I have been particularly impressed by the marked improvements in my ESL (English as a second language) students once I began incorporating online discussions, writing, and group collaboration into my curriculum. The volume of writing they did in our online discussions required that they express themselves clearly with words.

5. *Using technology creates a higher level of accountability and transparency.* Teachers can see who has done what in an online discussion or collaborative group work. The contributions of each group member are significantly easier to track and evaluate when the work is done online since there is an online transcript available.

This chapter provides suggestions to support teachers in assessing work done online to save them time and more actively engage students in self-reflection and peer editing. That said, there are times when a teacher will want to evaluate and assign a grade to work done online, so I have designed rubrics grounded in the Common Core State Standards for teachers to use to easily and efficiently evaluate online work.

Managing Online Participation

Most learning platforms and learning management systems (LMSs) have built-in reporting features that show user activity on the site. Some participation reports are more in depth, so this is another element to consider when you are selecting a learning platform.

A participation report makes it easy to see if a student has fulfilled the requirements for online work. For example, my Collaborize Classroom site allows me to print or export a variety of reports. The participation report is a general one that can be adjusted for any date range and tells me how many times each user has logged in, posted a comment, replied to a peer, and voted. I print out my participation report every 2 weeks to calculate participation points. I assign a value of 5 points for each response to a question or topic and 2 points for each substantive reply to a peer. This makes calculating their homework points a simple process.

I chose not to assign grades to the majority of the online work completed and instead opted for participation points. I wanted to encourage authentic exchanges between students, instead of long-winded postings attempting to impress me for a grade. I made it clear that I was more interested in the quality of the dialogue, not the quantity.

There were only a few instances when I would individually evaluate the online postings to assign a grade:

- *Individual contributions to a large-scale group assignment*
- *Selected creative writing assignments*
- *Formal writing that was posted for feedback*

Instead of grading individual postings, I spent my energy pulling out highlights from a discussion, identifying questions that needed to be answered in class, and designing student-centered extension activities to build on the work done online.

I also had more time to send individual messages via our Collaborize Classroom site to provide positive feedback and praise to students who were consistently adding value to our online conversations. Conversely, I sent messages to students who were not participating regularly or needed to develop their postings to more substantively contribute to the conversation. I was able to provide them with concrete strategies and direct them to resources to improve their online contributions.

I found that students were much more motivated to participate when they were interested in the topic or they knew the work in class was going to build directly on the work done online. This is the reason I have focused on designing creative student-centered activities to extend the boundaries of online discussions and assignments. If students look forward to class and know they will be expected to participate actively in the classroom, they are more likely to complete the work online. They will appreciate the purpose of work assigned, and you can answer the ever-present question "Why do we have to do this?" Weaving the work done in the online space with work done in the classroom will ultimately be the biggest incentive for the majority of students.

Even though I do not advocate for teachers to assign a grade evaluating the quality of every posting, I do feel it is important to give students points for participation. Some teachers allocate a percentage of the total grade for online work, while others assign a participation point value to each posting. It is a matter of personal preference. Regardless of your strategy for giving students credit for work completed online, it is important that you make those points visible to students since they are not getting papers handed back with scores on them. It can be easy for online work and points associated with that work to be out of sight, out of mind.

When I first transitioned to a blended learning model with online discussions, many students expressed concern about not knowing how many points they were earning online. I showed them how to check their own participation reports online, but many did not take the time to do this regularly. I realized I needed a strategy to make their points earned for online participation more visible. The following are three ways to make the point values visible for students.

1. *Create printed reports.* This can be done in a variety of ways, depending on your learning platform or LMS. Some LMSs have a grade book built into the system that students can view, which makes it easy for them to track their grade online.

Because many of my students did not regularly check their grades online, I designed the following printouts at the end of each 2-week period to hand to students to ensure they all knew how many participation points they had earned.

2. *Conference one-on-one with students.* Building in time during the school day once every 2–4 weeks to meet briefly with each student to discuss his or her performance online is another way to ensure they know how they are doing. If students are working in groups on a creative self-directed student-centered activity in class, it can provide the time needed to facilitate mini-conferences.

Online Participation
From: _____[date]_____ To: _____[date]_____
Responses: Required: _____ Posted: _____
Replies: Required: _____ Posted: _____
Total Points:
Comments:

This is also a good opportunity to make sure that inconsistent or infrequent participation is not due to a lack of access. As I stated earlier it is becoming increasingly important to find students access, but it can be hard to know if a student is having a problem if you don't ask. Many students may be hesitant to take the initiative and approach a teacher about an issue related to technology at home.

In my own experience, I have had students tell me that their parents had to turn off the Internet connection due to money issues or that a sibling monopolizes the one computer in the house. It is helpful when I know what is causing the issue because then I can problem solve with them. Do they have a free period in their schedule when they could go to the school library to use computers? Is there a local library near them where they can get online? Can they come by my room during lunch or break to jump online? Have they heard about programs that offer low-cost Internet and refurbished computers? These conversations have been really positive because students realize I want to support them and help them succeed.

3. *Have students self-assess and reflect.* Asking students to track and evaluate their own work online using participation reports puts a degree of responsibility on them. It can be helpful for them to review their online work in regular intervals, then reflect in writing about what they feel they have done well, what areas need

improvement, and where they see growth. Students rarely take the time to reflect on their work, so building this practice into your class can help them recognize their progress. When they see that they are in fact growing and improving, they appreciate and value their work more. This is a strategy that may be more appropriate for older students.

Rubrics

Using a consistent set of rubrics can help students see where they have developed over time. If they compare rubrics, they can see the elements that have improved. The rubrics I have designed for this section are meant to support teachers in evaluating work done online more easily. They are based on a 4-point scale for simplicity.

Teachers can print these rubrics and fill them out by hand or use these rubric criteria to create a form in Google Docs. Using a Google Docs form can make the process of evaluating work easier for a teacher with a large number of students. Information inserted into the form is then captured in a clear spreadsheet, saving teachers time when entering grades.

Online Discussion Rubric

http://goo.gl/UiCWQ

Element	Needs Improvement 1	Fair 2	Strong 3	Excellent 4
Addresses the Question	Fails to address all parts of the discussion question.	Addresses parts of the discussion question.	Addresses most aspects of the discussion question.	Thoroughly addresses all parts of the discussion question.
Substantive Nature of Post	Not substantive in nature.	Attempts a substantive response but needs more detail.	Substantive in nature with clear details and examples.	Substantive in nature. Added depth to the overall conversation.

Element	*Needs Improvement* 1	*Fair* 2	*Strong* 3	*Excellent* 4
Organization and Clarity	Lacks organization and is unclear.	Attempts organization, but writing in places is unclear.	Organized and clear.	Extremely organized and clear throughout.
Mechanics (Spelling and Grammar)	Distracting mechanical errors throughout.	Mechanical errors distract at times.	A couple errors present, but they do not distract.	Mechanics reflect careful editing.

Group Work Rubric

http://goo.gl/WiLqc

Element	*Needs Improvement* 1	*Fair* 2	*Strong* 3	*Excellent* 4
Completes the Task Assigned	Fails to complete all parts of the group task.	Addresses only parts of the group task.	Completes most of the group task.	All parts of the group task are completed thoroughly.
Quality of Contributions to the Group	Group work fails to meet minimum requirements.	Group work satisfies minimum requirements but lacks depth.	Quality of group work is strong, but there is room for further development.	Group work exceeds requirements and reflects hard work.
Communication and Cooperation With Peers	Students did not effectively communicate or cooperate, which negatively impacted the quality of work.	Students attempted to communicate, but cooperation at times needed improvement.	Students communicated and cooperated to accomplish tasks assigned.	Students effectively communicated and cooperated to achieve highest quality of work.
Mechanics (Spelling and Grammar)	Distracting mechanical errors throughout.	Mechanical errors distract at times.	A couple errors present, but they do not distract.	Mechanics reflect careful editing.

The writing rubrics are rooted in the Common Core State Standards, which emphasize argument, informative, and narrative writing. I have designed rubrics for each type of writing at each level: upper elementary, middle school, and high school. They may need to be adjusted slightly to best meet your needs. The language used is taken directly from the Standards and organized in categories based on the points of emphasis for each type of writing. I have also attempted to keep the language consistent as the rubrics progress from upper elementary through high school so students can recognize their development.

Upper Elementary Rubrics

Opinion Writing

http://goo.gl/6tS5W

Element	*Needs Improvement* 1	*Fair* 2	*Strong* 3	*Excellent* 4
Opinion With Reasons	Opinion is unclear; no reasons are given.	Opinion is clear, but reasons are unclear or incomplete.	Opinion is clearly stated, and reasons are stated.	Opinion is clearly stated, and reasons are strong.
Evidence	Opinion is not supported. No evidence is provided.	Attempts to support opinion and reasons with facts, but the information is unclear or inaccurate.	Supports opinion and reasons with facts and necessary details.	Supports opinion and reasons with strong, accurate facts and thorough details.
Explanation	Little to no explanation of the information presented.	Explanation attempts to discuss the information but is unclear at times.	Clear explanation that discusses most of the information presented.	Clear and concise explanation that thoroughly discusses the information presented.

Element	*Needs Improvement* 1	*Fair* 2	*Strong* 3	*Excellent* 4
Conclusion	Abrupt ending. No concluding statement.	Ends with a concluding statement that does not clearly relate to the opinion stated.	Ends with a concluding statement about the opinion stated.	Effectively ends with a strong concluding statement.
Organization and Transitions	Little to no attempt at organization.	Attempts to organize ideas, but transitional language needs to be added.	Organizes ideas in a logical way. Transitional language used.	Strong organization and transitional language used throughout.
Mechanics (Spelling and Grammar)	Distracting mechanical errors throughout.	Mechanical errors distract at times.	A couple errors present, but they do not distract	Mechanics reflect careful editing.

Informative/Explanatory Writing

http://goo.gl/dseq2

Element	*Needs Improvement* 1	*Fair* 2	*Strong* 3	*Excellent* 4
Topic	Topic is unclear.	Introduces topic, but focus is unclear.	Introduces the topic.	Clearly introduces the topic.
Evidence	Little to no facts, concrete details, quotations, or examples included.	Attempts to develop topic with facts and examples, but lacks quotations and concrete details.	Develops topic with facts, concrete details, quotations, and examples.	Thoroughly develops topic with important facts, concrete details, quotations, and examples.

(Continued)

(Continued)

Element	Needs Improvement 1	Fair 2	Strong 3	Excellent 4
Explanation	Little to no explanation of the information presented.	Explanation attempts to discuss the information but is unclear at times.	Clear explanation that discusses most of the information presented.	Clear and concise explanation that thoroughly discusses the information presented.
Conclusion	Abrupt ending. No concluding statement.	Ends with a concluding statement that does not clearly relate to topic.	Ends with a concluding statement about the topic.	Effectively ends with a strong concluding statement.
Organization and Transitions	Little to no attempt at organization.	Attempts to organize ideas, but transitional language needs to be added.	Organizes ideas in a logical way. Transitional language used.	Strong organization and transitional language used throughout.
Mechanics (Spelling and Grammar)	Distracting mechanical errors throughout.	Mechanical errors distract at times.	A couple errors present, but they do not distract.	Mechanics reflect careful editing.

Narrative Writing

http://goo.gl/3806B

Element	Needs Improvement 1	Fair 2	Strong 3	Excellent 4
Establishes Situation and Introduces Characters	Situation is unclear. Narrator is not introduced and characters are poorly developed.	Attempts to establish a situation. Introduces narrator and develops at least one character.	Establishes a situation, introduces the narrator, and develops characters.	Establishes a clear situation, introduces the narrator, and develops interesting characters.

Element	Needs Improvement 1	Fair 2	Strong 3	Excellent 4
Narrative Techniques	Little to no attempt to use dialogue, description, and pacing. Experiences and events are underdeveloped throughout.	Attempts to use dialogue, description, and pacing, but experiences and events are underdeveloped.	Uses dialogue, description, and pacing to develop experiences and events.	Effectively uses dialogue, description, and pacing to develop experiences and events.
Sequence of Events	Unclear sequence of events. Plot is hard to follow throughout.	Attempts to sequence events. Plot is hard to follow in places.	Clear sequence of events that unfold naturally.	Clear purposeful sequence of events that unfold naturally.
Conclusion	Abrupt ending. No concluding statement.	Ends with a concluding statement that does not clearly follow from the narrative.	Ends with a concluding statement that follows from the narrative.	Effectively ends with a strong concluding statement that follows from the narrative.
Organization and Transitions	Little to no attempt at organization.	Attempts to organize ideas, but transitional language needs to be added.	Organizes ideas in a logical way. Transitional language used.	Strong organization and transitional language used throughout.
Mechanics (Spelling and Grammar)	Distracting mechanical errors throughout.	Mechanical errors distract at times.	A couple errors present, but they do not distract.	Mechanics reflect careful editing.

Middle School Rubrics

Argument Writing

http://goo.gl/m5Cyk

(Continued)

(Continued)

Element	Needs Improvement 1	Fair 2	Strong 3	Excellent 4
Clear Claim With Reasons	Claim(s) is unclear. No clear reasons are given.	Claim(s) is clear, but reasons are absent or incomplete.	Claim(s) is clearly stated and reasons are stated.	Claim(s) is clearly stated and reasons are strong.
Evidence	Claim(s) is not supported. No evidence provided.	Attempts to support claim(s) and reasons with facts, but information is unclear and/or inaccurate.	Supports claim(s) and reasons with facts and necessary details.	Supports claim(s) and reasons with strong, accurate facts and thorough details.
Explanation	Little to no explanation of the information presented.	Explanation attempts to discuss the information but is unclear at times.	Clear explanation that discusses most of the information presented.	Clear and concise explanation that thoroughly discusses the information presented.
Conclusion	Abrupt ending. No concluding statement.	Ends with a concluding statement that does not clearly relate to argument.	Ends with a concluding statement about the argument presented.	Effectively ends with a strong concluding statement.
Formal Tone and Style	Informal language present throughout.	Writing contains some informal elements (e.g., contractions).	Writing attempts to maintain a formal and objective tone.	Writing maintains a formal and objective tone throughout.
Organization and Transitions	Little to no attempt at organization.	Attempts to organize ideas, but transitional language needs to be added.	Organizes ideas in a logical way. Transitional language used.	Strong organization and transitional language used throughout.
Mechanics (Spelling and Grammar)	Distracting mechanical errors throughout.	Mechanical errors distract at times.	A couple errors present, but they do not distract.	Mechanics reflect careful editing.

Informative Writing

http://goo.gl/bTIOm

Element	Needs Improvement 1	Fair 2	Strong 3	Excellent 4
Topic	Topic is unclear.	Introduces topic, but the focus and main points are unclear.	Introduces the topic and previews main points.	Clearly introduces the topic and previews main points.
Evidence	Little to no facts, concrete details, quotations, or examples included.	Attempts to develop topic with facts, concrete details, and examples, but some information is not relevant.	Develops topic with facts, concrete details, quotations, and examples.	Thoroughly develops topic with well-chosen facts, concrete details, quotations, and examples.
Explanation	Little to no explanation of the information presented.	Explanation attempts to discuss the information but is unclear at times.	Clear explanation that discusses most of the information presented.	Clear and concise explanation that thoroughly discusses the information presented.
Conclusion	Abrupt ending. No concluding statement.	Ends with a concluding statement that does not clearly relate to topic.	Ends with a concluding statement about the topic.	Effectively ends with a strong concluding statement.
Formal Tone and Style	Informal language present throughout.	Writing contains some informal elements (e.g., contractions).	Writing attempts to maintain a formal and objective tone.	Writing maintains a formal and objective tone throughout.
Organization and Transitions	Little to no attempt at organization.	Attempts to organize ideas, but transitional language needs to be added.	Organizes ideas in a logical way. Transitional language used.	Strong organization and transitional language used throughout.
Mechanics (Spelling and Grammar)	Distracting mechanical errors throughout.	Mechanical errors distract at times.	A couple errors present, but they do not distract.	Mechanics reflect careful editing.

Narrative Writing

http://goo.gl/CN2nJ

Element	Needs Improvement 1	Fair 2	Strong 3	Excellent 4
Orients and Engages the Reader	Does not engage or orient reader. Situation is unclear. Narrator is not introduced and characters are poorly developed.	Attempts to engage the reader by establishing a situation. Introduces narrator and develops at least one character.	Engages and orients the reader by establishing a situation, introducing the narrator, and developing characters.	Immediately engages and orients the reader by establishing a clear situation, introducing the narrator, and developing interesting characters.
Narrative Techniques	Little to no attempt to use dialogue, description, and pacing. Experiences and events are underdeveloped throughout.	Attempts to use dialogue, description, and pacing, but experiences, events, and/or characters are underdeveloped.	Uses dialogue, description, and pacing to develop experiences, events, and characters.	Effectively uses dialogue, description, and pacing to develop experiences, events, and characters.
Sequence of Events	Unclear sequence of events. Plot is hard to follow throughout.	Attempts to sequence events. Plot is hard to follow in places.	Clear sequence of events that unfold naturally.	Clear purposeful sequence of events that unfold naturally.
Conclusion	Abrupt ending. No concluding statement.	Ends with a concluding statement that does not clearly follow from the narrative.	Ends with a concluding statement that follows from the narrative.	Effectively ends with a strong concluding statement that follows from the narrative.

Element	Needs Improvement 1	Fair 2	Strong 3	Excellent 4
Organization and Transitions	Little to no attempt at organization.	Attempts to organize ideas, but transitional language needs to be added.	Organizes ideas in a logical way. Transitional language used.	Strong organization and transitional language used throughout.
Mechanics (Spelling and Grammar)	Distracting mechanical errors throughout.	Mechanical errors distract at times.	A couple errors present, but they do not distract.	Mechanics reflect careful editing.

High School Rubrics

Argument Writing

http://goo.gl/s6Pzb

Element	Needs Improvement 1	Fair 2	Strong 3	Excellent 4
Clear Claim With Reasons	Claim(s) is unclear; no clear reasons are given.	Claim(s) is clear, but reasons are absent or incomplete.	Claim(s) is clearly stated and reasons are stated.	Claim(s) is clearly stated and reasons are strong.
Evidence	Claim(s) is not supported. No evidence provided.	Attempts to support claim(s) and reasons with facts, but information is unclear and/or inaccurate.	Supports claim(s) and reasons with facts and necessary details.	Supports claim(s) and reasons with strong, accurate facts and thorough details.

(Continued)

(Continued)

Element	Needs Improvement 1	Fair 2	Strong 3	Excellent 4
Explanation	Little explanation and no analysis of the information presented.	Explanation attempts to discuss the information but is unclear at times.	Clear explanation that discusses most of the information presented.	Clear and concise explanation that thoroughly discusses the information presented.
Conclusion	Abrupt ending. No concluding statement.	Ends with a concluding statement that does not clearly relate to argument.	Ends with a concluding statement about the argument presented.	Effectively ends with a strong concluding statement.
Formal Tone and Style	Informal language present throughout.	Writing contains some informal elements (e.g., contractions).	Writing attempts to maintain a formal and objective tone.	Writing maintains a formal and objective tone throughout.
Organization and Transitions	Little to no attempt at organization.	Attempts to organize ideas, but transitional language needs to be added.	Organizes ideas in a logical way. Transitional language used.	Strong organization and transitional language used throughout.
Mechanics (Spelling and Grammar)	Distracting mechanical errors throughout.	Mechanical errors distract at times.	A couple errors present, but they do not distract.	Mechanics reflect careful editing.

Informative Writing

http://goo.gl/mYE7B

Element	Needs Improvement 1	Fair 2	Strong 3	Excellent 4
Topic	Topic is unclear.	Introduces topic, but the focus and main points are unclear.	Introduces the topic and previews main points.	Clearly introduces the topic and previews main points.
Evidence	Little to no facts, concrete details, quotations, or examples included.	Attempts to develop topic with facts, concrete details, and examples, but some information is not relevant.	Develops topic with well-chosen facts, concrete details, quotations, and examples.	Thoroughly develops topic with significant and relevant facts, concrete details, quotations, and examples.
Explanation	Little to no explanation of the information presented.	Explanation and analysis attempt to discuss the information, but ideas do not build on each other clearly.	Clear explanation and analysis that examine most of the information presented.	Clear, concise explanation and thorough analysis that examine all parts of the information presented.
Conclusion	Abrupt ending. No concluding statement.	Ends with a concluding statement that does not clearly relate to the topic.	Ends with a concluding statement about the topic.	Effectively ends with a strong concluding statement that supports explanation.
Formal Tone and Style	Informal language present throughout.	Writing contains some informal elements (e.g., contractions).	Writing attempts to maintain a formal and objective tone.	Writing maintains a formal and objective tone throughout.
Organization and Transitions	Little to no attempt at organization.	Attempts to organize ideas, but transitional language needs to be added.	Organizes ideas in a logical way. Transitional language used.	Strong organization and transitional language used throughout.
Mechanics (Spelling and Grammar)	Distracting mechanical errors throughout.	Mechanical errors distract at times.	A couple errors present, but they do not distract.	Mechanics reflect careful editing.

Narrative Writing

http://goo.gl/aXkF9

Element	Needs Improvement 1	Fair 2	Strong 3	Excellent 4
Orients and Engages the Reader	Does not engage or orient reader. Situation, problem, or observation is unclear. Narrator and/or characters are poorly developed.	Attempts to engage the reader by establishing a situation, problem, or observation. Introduces narrator and develops at least one character.	Engages and orients the reader by establishing a situation, problem, or observation. Introduces the narrator and develops characters.	Immediately engages and orients the reader. Establishes a clear situation, problem, or observation. Introduces the narrator and develops interesting characters.
Narrative Techniques	Little to no attempt to use dialogue, description, and pacing. Experiences and events are underdeveloped throughout.	Attempts to use dialogue, description, and pacing, but experiences, events, and/or characters are underdeveloped.	Uses dialogue, description, and pacing to develop experiences, events, and characters.	Effectively uses dialogue, description, and pacing to develop experiences, events, and characters.
Sequence of Events	Unclear sequence of events. Plot is hard to follow throughout.	Attempts to sequence events. Plot is hard to follow in places.	Clear sequence of events that unfold naturally.	Clear purposeful sequence of events that unfold naturally.
Conclusion	Abrupt ending. No concluding statement.	Ends with a concluding statement that does not clearly follow from the narrative.	Ends with a concluding statement that follows from the narrative.	Effectively ends with a strong concluding statement that follows from the narrative.

Element	Needs Improvement 1	Fair 2	Strong 3	Excellent 4
Organization and Transitions	Little to no attempt at organization.	Attempts to organize ideas, but transitional language needs to be added.	Organizes ideas in a logical way. Transitional language used.	Strong organization and transitional language used throughout.
Mechanics (Spelling and Grammar)	Distracting mechanical errors throughout.	Mechanical errors distract at times.	A couple errors present, but they do not distract.	Mechanics reflect careful editing.

Teachers can use forms in Google Docs or a tool like Rubistar, an online rubric-making tool, to design rubrics that best meet their needs. Rubrics can be made for a variety of assignments, activities, writing tasks, and so on, and they can be printed or saved to an online account for future use.

Rubistar

rubistar.4teachers.org

Design rubrics for a variety of assignments, print, and save.

Free

Preparing Students for High-Stakes Exams

A chapter on assessment would not be complete without a discussion of the standardized exams that are being given to assess both student performance and teacher effectiveness. Love them or hate them, standardized exams are a part of the education culture in our country. I, personally, do not believe that standardized exams are an accurate measure of either student knowledge or teacher ability. That said, if my students are being judged based on their performance on these exams, then I feel I have a responsibility to prepare them. I do not want to use "drill and kill" review methods to raise test scores, but I do want to familiarize my students with the language and questions they will encounter on these exams.

When I adopted a blended instruction model, I decided to use my Collaborize Classroom site to post released test questions from the California High School Exit Exam, Standardized Testing and Reporting, and SAT. My objective was to present questions for students to read and discuss. The focus was not on getting the "right answer" but rather on encouraging a dialogue about the questions and how students arrived at an answer. I encouraged them to share tips and strategies when they successfully answered a question. Conversely, I encouraged them to ask questions and identify parts of the problems they didn't understand or vocabulary that was unfamiliar. I hoped that if students saw the questions as problems to be solved, instead of being scared or intimidated by them, they would experience less anxiety during these exams and, ultimately, be more successful.

At the beginning of second semester, I started introducing a test-taking tip each day in class. We would discuss it and I would walk through an example in class. Then I would post a released question online using the multiple-choice question type. Students were required to select an answer and explain how they arrived at their answer—sharing any strategies they used to answer the question. The next day, I would publish the question to the Results Page and provide the correct answer. We would discuss the results to identify incorrect answers and highlight strong tips and strategies shared.

Standardized Exam Preparation

A blended instruction approach made it possible to introduce my students to test-taking tips in class, make practice questions available online to motivate discussion, then weave those discussions back into the classroom without sacrificing large amounts of class time. It made test preparation a short daily practice.

Several students approached me after "testing season" was over and thanked me for taking the time to provide test-taking tips and practice questions. They said they encountered many of the vocabulary words/academic language we covered in our discussions. They also commented on how helpful it was to know what to expect on the exams since the questions were familiar.

Released Test Questions Online

The College Board website is a great resource for both test-taking tips and practice questions. The practice questions are preceded by "general hints" such as "Select the choice that best answers the question asked. Don't select a choice just because it is a true statement." These are the types of hints or tips I would introduce in class and have students record in the "Test-Taking Tips" section of their notebooks for future reference. I have included a list of the test-taking tips I share with my own students (see below). These are strategies I have gathered over the years in my work preparing students for standardized exams. I hope they will be helpful to other educators preparing students for standardized exams.

I recommended to students that they save these tips and study them in preparation for the SAT, which was a test many of them were most concerned about. I explained that state-mandated tests were great practice for the SAT because they could use the tips they had learned and strategies they had identified in our discussions to improve their test taking in general.

Tucker's Test-Taking Tips for English Language Arts

1. *General.* Work on sentence completion and grammar questions first. They take less time than the passage-based reading questions.

2. *Reading a Passage.* Always read the question before reading the passage. Identify one to three key words in each question. Then look for those key words and phrases as you read the passage.

3. *Reading Two Passages.* Do *not* jump from passage to passage. Stay with a passage until you have answered as many of the questions as you can before moving to the next passage. Remember to "leave tracks in the snow" on the passage by actively annotating and making brief notes to yourself so it is easier to return to a passage and answer questions if you have time at the end of a section.

(Continued)

(Continued)

4. *Sentence Completion (With Two Blanks).* When answering sentence completion questions with two blanks (two words omitted), always focus on one blank at a time. If any of the words do not fit in that blank, then you can eliminate that entire choice from consideration.

5. *Sentence Completion.* Read the sentence carefully for meaning. Think about what the sentence means and what part of speech is necessary to correctly complete the sentence.

6. *Sentence Completion.* Think of an answer that makes sense before you read the choices, then look for an answer in the choices that is similar to the answer you came up with on your own. What word or words could complete the sentence? You may see your choice or a similar choice in the possible answers. This exercise will help you analyze the sentence and, should your choice not be found in the answer choices, begin to reexamine the question in case you misinterpreted the clue word.

7. *Sentence Completion.* Be on the lookout for clue words. These indicate the types of answer choices that will best fit in the sentence and can indicate directional changes to the sentences' structures. These are some examples of clue words:

   - however
   - because
   - although
   - so
   - but

   Every SAT sentence has at least one clue word. Nearly every answer choice will appear correct if you do not find the clue word. This is why it is so imperative that you find the clue words before you look at the answer choices. Watch out for negative clue words such as *not, none,* and words that begin with *un-.*

8. *Sentence Completion (With Two Blanks).* Use the process of elimination. This is especially true of the questions with two blanks. This essentially doubles the chance that you will know at least one of the two words in the answer choices and that you can eliminate the choice from consideration if the words do not make sense. By eliminating the wrong answers, you may find you are left with only one possible correct answer.

9. *Reading Passage.* Read a line above and a line below those specified in the question. This will ensure that you catch the entire context of the reading relating to the question. Expect to see incorrect answers that seek to exploit those test takers who do not read these additional lines.

10. *Sentence Completion.* Always read all answer choices. All standardized exams want you to select the *best* answer choice in the sentence completion section. And if you are strapped for time and you select A because it works without checking the other choices, it just may be that E was an even better selection.

Tucker's Test-Taking Tips for Math

1. Before beginning the first question, write down all the formulas you can remember, even the "easy" ones.

2. Come up with your own answer before looking at the answer choices. If your answer is way off, you will notice and be able to correct it.

3. Show your work. Even though it may not be a factor in your grade, it helps you avoid making simple mistakes or skipping necessary steps.

4. Do not get hung up on a difficult problem. If you get stuck, skip it and come back if you have time. Other problems may help jog your memory.

5. If you are stuck, try substituting an answer you think is correct for the variables in the question. Do this only after you have eliminated two or three answers because you will not have time to do this with all the possible answers.

6. Schedule a maximum amount of time for each problem. Problems at the beginning are often tricky but quick. You should be able to answer them in a few seconds. You may, however, want to set a limit on how long you spend on the more difficult, time-consuming problems.

7. Start wherever you feel comfortable, and do not hesitate to skip around. Doing the easy problems first will help build your confidence and ensure that you have plenty of time for the more labor-intensive ones. Remember to circle the numbers of any problems you skip.

(Continued)

(Continued)

8. Clearly label all parts of diagrams or graphs. Putting all the related information you know down on paper may help you solve a problem.

9. Before you begin answering a question with a chart or graphic organizer, write down all the information you can learn from it. Pull out only the facts you need to solve a given problem since extra information will create confusion.

10. When there are many possible solutions to a problem, figure out minimum and maximum values before even looking at the answers. Often, only one of the answers will fit in the possible range.

Teacher's Note: For more tips, strategies, and released questions, check out the College Board website: www.collegeboard.com/student/testing/psat/prep.html.

Sharing these tips with students and providing them with multiple opportunities to work with released test questions from past exams will boost their confidence and lower their affective filters on test day. The discussion component of online test preparation can empower students to problem solve, ask questions, and share strategies that will make them more successful when they are navigating a timed exam.

Chapter Summary

Assessing student work online can be done in a variety of ways, and each teacher must decide on the assessment strategy that works best for them. A teacher using a learning platform or LMS to engage students outside of the classroom must decide on a method of assigning points for work completed online that does not add to their workload. In an attempt to lighten the workload for teachers, I encourage them to give participation credit/points for the majority of work done online, instead of attempting to grade and evaluate every posting or assignment. This communicates to students that teachers value the work done online, but it does not add substantially to their grading. In the long term, tapping into student interest, using the online work to drive the work done in class, and helping students recognize their own growth will be more motivating than a grade.

A teacher who is not attempting to grade every contribution to the online conversations can spend that energy designing student-centered activities and reflecting on his or her teaching/methodology. Teachers who take homework online using online discussions and collaborative group work will find that they have more time to spend on the aspects of teaching that they enjoy.

There are some discussions, group work, and writing assignments that a teacher may want to grade. I designed a set of rubrics anchored in the Common Core State Standards for teachers to use that will make it easy for students to see their progress over time.

Online discussions can provide the time and space to prepare students for standardized exams without sacrificing precious class time. Posting released test questions online for students to discuss exposes them to vocabulary and question types they will encounter on standardized exams. It also gives them an opportunity to share tips and strategies for finding the answer to questions.

Book Study Questions

1. What percentage of your total time spent on schoolwork is consumed by grading? How much time do you spend designing creative hands-on activities? How much time do you spend each week reflecting on your teaching practices and methodology? How much time do you spend each month exploring new technology, reading other educators' blogs, or attending professional development? As you consider how you spend your time, think about what you would most enjoy doing. How could transitioning to a blended instruction model create more time for you to focus on the aspects of teaching that interest you most?

2. What does your typical homework assignment look like right now? How do you grade the homework your students complete? How much time do you spend preparing, grading, and entering scores for homework? How could you use online discussions and group work to save time grading paperwork?

3. When students in your class have a question, do they typically ask a classmate or you? If they ask you, what strategies can you use to shift this norm so they ask one another first? Why is it important for students to see each other as valuable resources?

4. What do you think will best motivate your students to participate in online discussions and group work in the long term? How can you use that knowledge to design both online and in-class activities that will inspire them to actively participate?

5. What strategy for assessing work online would you use to ensure that integrating an online component will save you time? Do you have concerns about how you would assess online work? If so, what are they? How might you address these concerns?

6. How would you make the points earned online visible to students? What point values would you attribute to responses to questions versus replies to peers? Are there assignments you would want to grade as opposed to giving participation points? If so, how would you provide feedback to students?

7. How would using a consistent set of rubrics when grading online discussions, group work, and/or writing benefit students? How would rubrics make it easier for students to provide each other with focused feedback? How might rubrics be used to facilitate self-reflection to encourage students to look at their work more closely?

8. Which standardized exams are required in your state? How do you currently prepare students for these exams? How could you use a blended instruction approach to give students more practice without sacrificing class time? Do you think it would be beneficial for students to discuss questions and strategies?

Index

CORWIN

A SAGE Company

The Corwin logo—a raven striding across an open book—represents the union of courage and learning. Corwin is committed to improving education for all learners by publishing books and other professional development resources for those serving the field of PreK–12 education. By providing practical, hands-on materials, Corwin continues to carry out the promise of its motto: **"Helping Educators Do Their Work Better."**